THE POET'S CAT

An Anthology compiled by
MONA GOODEN

With a Frontispiece engraved by
STEPHEN GOODEN

Granger Index Reprint Series

BOOKS FOR LIBRARIES PRESS
FREEPORT, NEW YORK

First published 1946
by George G. Harrap & Co., Ltd.
Copyright. All rights reserved
Reprinted 1969 by arrangement

TO
MY MOTHER
WITH LOVE

LIBRARY OF CONGRESS CATALOG CARD NUMBER:
74-75711

MANUFACTURED
BY
HALLMARK LITHOGRAPHERS, INC.
IN THE U.S.A.

ACKNOWLEDGMENTS

For permission to include in this anthology copyright poems my grateful thanks are due to the following:

Professor Claude Colleer Abbott and Messrs Chatto and Windus for " Bunch: a Cat," from *Miss Bedell and other Poems*; Mr William Rose Benét for " Street of Cats " and " Bast "; Mr Joseph Braddock and the *Observer* for " Black Cat in Prunustree "; Dr Maurice James Craig for " High on a Ridge of Tiles " and " Three Cat Poems "; Mrs Frances Cornford for " On Maou dying at the Age of Six Months "; Mr R. N. Currey and the *Dublin Magazine* for a translation of Du Bellay's " Epitaphe d'un Chat "; Mr Walter de la Mare and Messrs Faber and Faber, Ltd., for " Five Eyes "; Mr Oliver Edwards and the *Welsh Review* for " The Cat and the Man "; Mr T. S. Eliot and Messrs Faber and Faber, Ltd., for " Macavity: the Mystery Cat," from *Old Possum's Book of Practical Cats*; Dr Robin Flower and Messrs Constable and Co., Ltd., for " Pangur Bán "; Mr Alexander Gray and Messrs Faber and Faber, Ltd., for " On a Cat Aging," from *Gossip* ; Messrs William Heinemann, Ltd., for " Epitaph on the Duchess of Maine's Cat " and a quotation from a poem of Pierre de Ronsard, both translated by Sir Edmund Gosse; the Trustees of the Hardy Estate, and Messrs Macmillan and Co., Ltd., for " Last Words to a Dumb Friend," by Thomas Hardy; Messrs George Allen and Unwin, Ltd., for " Mike " and " To a Persian Cat," from *Fritto Misto*, by F. C. W. Hiley; Messrs Michael Joseph, Ltd., for " To a Siamese Cat," from *Charles: the Story of a Friendship*, by Michael Joseph; Miss Ethna MacCarthy and the *Dublin Magazine* for " The Shrine "; Mr D. S. MacColl for a translation of " Les Chats," by Baudelaire; Mr D. S. MacColl and Messrs Basil Blackwell, Ltd., for " Connoisseurs "; Sir Edward Marsh and Messrs William Heinemann, Ltd., for " Cat into Lady " and " The Cat and the Fox," both translated from La Fontaine; Miss Eva Martin for " Cat and Crocuses "; Mrs Alida Monro and the Poetry Bookshop for " Milk for the Cat " and " Cat's Meat," by Harold Monro; Mr Cedric Morris and

Wales for "Passage on"; Mr Seumas O'Sullivan for "Tony's Grave," "Epitaphium Felis," and "Le Petit Chat" (the last two poems translated respectively from Jortin and Rostand); Mr Herbert Palmer and Messrs J. M. Dent and Sons, Ltd., for "Phil, the Black Persian," from *Collected Poems*; Miss Ruth Pitter and the Cresset Press, Ltd., for "The Kitten's Eclogue" and "The Matron Cat's Song," from *A Mad Lady's Garland*; Miss Ruth Pitter and *Lilliput* for "Quorum Porum" and "The Safety-valve"; the Hon. V. Sackville-West and the Hogarth Press for "The Greater Cats"; Miss Dorothy Sayers and *Time and Tide* for "War Cat"; Mr Michael Scot for "Kittens," "Charcoal Sketch," "Ballad of the Cats of Bygone Time," and four lines from a poem quoted in the Introduction; Dr W. Bedell Stanford for "The Cat and the Partridge"; Sir Edward Marsh and Mr James Strachey for "The Cat," by Lytton Strachey; Messrs William Heinemann, Ltd., for "To a Cat," by A. C. Swinburne, and also for "Cat and Lady," a translation from Verlaine by Arthur Symons; Mrs Helen Thomas and Messrs Faber and Faber, Ltd., for "A Cat," by Edward Thomas; Dr Tritton for his translation from the Arabic, "Hungry Master and Hungry Cat"; Messrs John Lane, the Bodley Head, Ltd., for "To my Cat" and "Arsinoë's Cats," from *Poems* by Rosamund Marriott Watson; and Mrs W. B. Yeats and Messrs Macmillan and Co, Ltd., for "The Cat and the Moon," from *The Collected Poems of W. B. Yeats*.

I must also specially thank those friends who have helped me with various suggestions, particularly Mrs Joan Rhoades, Mrs Emilia Stuart Williamson, Sir Edward Marsh, Mr Michael Scot, and Mr Seumas O'Sullivan, who, both as poet and bibliographer, has encouraged me throughout.

M. G.

CONTENTS

Introduction   page 13

The Cat and the Partridge   23
    DAMOCHARIS THE GRAMMARIAN (*translated from the Greek by W. Bedell Stanford*)

Pangur Bán   23
    ANONYMOUS (*translated from the Irish by Dr Robin Flower*)

Hungry Master and Hungry Cat   24
    ABU SHAMAQMAQ (*translated from the Arabic by Dr A. S. Tritton*)

To a Cat   25
    IBN ALALAF ALNAHARWANY (*translated from the Arabic by J. D. Carlyle*)

Epitaph on a Pet Cat   26
    JOACHIM DU BELLAY (*translated from the French by R. N. Currey*)

The Lover, whose Mistresse feared a Mouse, declareth that he would become a Cat if he might have his Desire   32
    GEORGE TURBERVILLE

Epitaph on the Duchess of Maine's Cat   33
    LA MOTHE LE VAYER (*translated from the French by Sir Edmund Gosse*)

Cat into Lady   33
    JEAN DE LA FONTAINE (*translated from the French by Sir Edward Marsh*)

The Cat and the Fox   34
    JEAN DE LA FONTAINE (*translated from the French by Sir Edward Marsh*)

To my Lord Buckhurst, very Young, playing with a Cat   36
    MATTHEW PRIOR

Upon a Friend's Pet Cat, being Sick   36
    JOHN WINSTANLEY

The Rat-catcher and Cats JOHN GAY	page 39
Lisy's Parting with her Cat JAMES THOMSON	41
On the Death of a Favourite Cat, drowned in a Tub of Gold Fishes THOMAS GRAY	43
The Cat CHRISTOPHER SMART	44
The Retired Cat WILLIAM COWPER	45
The Colubriad WILLIAM COWPER	49
Familiarity Dangerous VINCENT BOURNE (*translated from the Latin by William Cowper*)	50
An Ode to Eight Cats belonging to Israel Mendez, a Jew "PETER PINDAR" (JOHN WOLCOT)	51
Epitaphium Felis JOHN JORTIN (*translated from the Latin by Seumas O'Sullivan*)	52
The Kitten JOANNA BAILLIE	52
The Kitten and Falling Leaves WILLIAM WORDSWORTH	56
Verses on a Cat PERCY BYSSHE SHELLEY	60
To a Cat JOHN KEATS	61
Cats CHARLES BAUDELAIRE (*translated from the French by D. S. MacColl*)	61
Atossa MATTHEW ARNOLD	62

Lays of Tom-cat Hiddigeigei   page 62
    J. V. SCHEFFEL (*translated from the German by W. Fitzgerald*)

On the Death of a Cat, a Friend of Mine aged Ten Years and a Half   64
    CHRISTINA ROSSETTI

To a Cat   65
    ALGERNON CHARLES SWINBURNE

Last Words to a Dumb Friend   67
    THOMAS HARDY

Cat and Lady   69
    PAUL VERLAINE (*translated from the French by Arthur Symons*)

Connoisseurs   70
    D. S. MACCOLL

To my Cat   70
    ROSAMUND MARRIOTT WATSON

Arsinoë's Cats   71
    ROSAMUND MARRIOTT WATSON

The Cat and the Moon   72
    WILLIAM BUTLER YEATS

Le Petit Chat   72
    EDMOND ROSTAND (*translated from the French by Seumas O'Sullivan*)

Five Eyes   74
    WALTER DE LA MARE

Tony's Grave   74
    SEUMAS O'SULLIVAN

A Cat   75
    EDWARD THOMAS

Milk for the Cat   76
    HAROLD MONRO

Cat's Meat   77
    HAROLD MONRO

The Cat   page 78
    LYTTON STRACHEY

Phil, the Black Persian   79
    HERBERT PALMER

On a Cat Aging   80
    ALEXANDER GRAY

Cat and Crocuses   81
    EVA MARTIN

On Maou dying at the Age of Six Months   81
    FRANCES CORNFORD

Street of Cats   81
    WILLIAM ROSE BENÉT

Bast   84
    WILLIAM ROSE BENÉT

Macavity : the Mystery Cat   84
    T. S. ELIOT

Bunch : a Cat   86
    CLAUDE COLLEER ABBOTT

Passage on   88
    CEDRIC MORRIS

Cat of Cats   88
    VIVIEN BULKLEY

To a Persian Cat   89
    F. C. W. HILEY

Mike   90
    F. C. W. HILEY

Kittens   92
    MICHAEL SCOT

Charcoal Sketch   93
    MICHAEL SCOT

The Greater Cats   94
    V. SACKVILLE-WEST

War Cat DOROTHY L. SAYERS	*page* 95
To a Siamese Cat MICHAEL JOSEPH	98
The Kitten's Eclogue RUTH PITTER	99
The Matron Cat's Song RUTH PITTER	100
Quorum Porum RUTH PITTER	102
The Safety-valve RUTH PITTER	103
The Cat and the Man OLIVER EDWARDS	104
Black Cat in Prunus-tree JOSEPH BRADDOCK	106
High on a Ridge of Tiles MAURICE JAMES CRAIG	107
Three Cat Poems MAURICE JAMES CRAIG	108
The Shrine ETHNA MACCARTHY	108
Nursery Rhymes	110
Ballad of the Cats of Bygone Time MICHAEL SCOT	113
Index of Authors	115

INTRODUCTION

As a domestic pet the cat has never enjoyed the popularity of the dog; yet between poets and their cats, with few exceptions, a natural sympathy seems always to have existed. This is not surprising, for both cat and poet are solitary, reserved, independent, and lovers of peaceful surroundings, and both possess the priceless gift of knowing how to amuse themselves when alone:

> We two are never bored together within the house,
> That is the absolute and eternal joke of it,
> Patiently I wait on knowledge, he, on a mouse,
> He sharpens up his claws whilst I polish my wit.

In almost the earliest poem included in this collection, which was written by an anonymous Irish monk in the eighth century, this friendship between writer and cat is most evident. Many early Irish poems show a strong observation of and delight in the natural world, its birds, beasts, and flowers; but few in such an intimate, individual way as in " Pangur Bán." Dr Flower, in his translation, has wonderfully conveyed the writer's innocent and poetic spirit, and the poem gives a vivid impression, as clear and bright as a medieval painting, of the scholar and his cat both so busy in the quiet cell of the monastery. There is another point of interest about this poem. Whether it was that he was a holy man, and therefore immune from popular superstition, or that he lived in Ireland, whence witches were believed to have been banished by St Patrick, the fact remains that the writer was unaffected by the bad reputation of cats in the Middle Ages as being the familiars of sorcerers of both sexes.

It is a striking proof of the strong personality of the cat, and of his power to inspire love or hatred, that he has in different ages and countries been worshipped or persecuted. In ancient Egypt, where cats were sacred to the goddess Bubastis, the penalty for killing a cat was death; and Herodotus tells us that when one died in a private house all the inhabitants shaved their eyebrows as a symbol of mourning. One has only to observe the cats embalmed in mummy cases, and preserved in the British

Museum and elsewhere, to conclude how much they were loved and valued while alive.

The horrible tortures inflicted on the feline race in medieval times, and even as late as the eighteenth century, when in the various Hell-fire Clubs of England and Ireland black cats were roasted alive, are too appalling to dwell upon. It is not surprising that after this strange and eventful history cats evoke such strong diversity of feelings in whatever company they are discussed.

Not all poets have loved them, however. In the earliest reference I can find in English literature, from the Prologue to "The Wyf of Bathe's Tale," in the *Canterbury Tales* (1386), Chaucer would seem to stress the vanity of the cat, as well as suggesting a less gentle alternative to buttering its paws:

> Thou seydest this, that I was lyk a cat;
> For whoso wolde senge a cattes skin,
> Thanne wolde the cat wel dwellen in his in;
> And if the cattes skin be slyk and gay,
> She wol nat dwelle in house half a day;
> But forth she wole, er any day be dawed,
> To shewe hir skin, and goon a-caterwawed.

Robert Henryson, from whose poem entitled "The Tale of the Uplands Mouse and the Burgess Mouse" (*c.* 1450) comes the next earliest mention, would appear to have regarded his pet with a more indulgent eye:

> And to the board they went, and togidder sat,
> And scantly had they drunken anis or twice,
> When in come Gib-hunter, our jolly cat,
> And bad God-speed: the Burgess up at that
> And til her hole she went as fire on flint.

In the plays of Shakespeare we find many uncomplimentary references to cats, among which are the following:

> I could endure anything before but a cat.
> *All's Well that Ends Well*, IV, iii
> Some, that are mad if they behold a cat.
> *The Merchant of Venice*, IV, i
> I am as vigilant as a cat to steal cream.
> *King Henry IV*, Pt. I, IV, ii

The French poet Pierre de Ronsard also had a low opinion of the feline clan:

> There is no man now living anywhere
> Who hates cats with a deeper hate than I;
> I hate their eyes, their heads, the way they stare,
> And when I see one come I turn and fly.

This was evidently an instinctive and temperamental dislike, but there have been other poets who had a definite reason for their antagonism, and almost always one finds that the detested animal has killed a pet bird. In Skelton's " Lament for Philip Sparrow " there is such a passage:

> Vengeance I ask and cry
> By way of exclamation,
> On all the whole nation
> Of cattes wild and tame . . .
>
> O cat of churlish kind,
> The fiend was in thy mind
> When thou my bird untwined;
> I would thou hadst been blind!

The same *motif* recurs in many other poems, such as " The Cat and the Partridge," from the Palatine Anthology, and " The Cat," by Edward Thomas.

These hate poems are natural enough, but should be regarded in their proper perspective. No doubt if one cherished a pet snail one would detest the bird who battered it to pieces on a stone before devouring it. Human beings batten on cows, sheep, pigs, and birds of every description, not always mercifully killed either; and when one considers the mass slaughter and cold-blooded tortures inflicted by men on each other in our time it would be mere extravagance to dwell unduly on the occasional cruelty of the cat.

Apart from invective, poems about cats would seem to fall into three classes. The first is the fabulist group. In the poems of La Fontaine and Gay the cats, like all the other animals, are symbols used by their authors to point a moral. Although they are often fantastic, as in " Cat into Lady," and endowed with human speech like the cats in fairy-tales, they do not possess the vivid personal appeal of Puss-in-boots, for example. We can never forget that they are puppets used by the puppet-master for his own ends, and not a hero or heroine with whose enthralling magical adventures our feelings become involved ; for the fable, unlike the fairy-tale, is a supremely intellectual and satirical literary genre, and it is for their pointed wit, and acute observation of human nature in all its fallibility and folly, that we read La Fontaine, John Gay, and others.

The second group appear to concentrate on the more obvious and less attractive characteristics of the cat, such as its curiosity, greed for fish, and love of comfort. Neither Cowper, in his poem " The Retired Cat," nor Gray, in his famous " Cat drowned in a Tub of Gold Fishes," displays any feeling for his pet, other than a reflective and somewhat wry amusement at its predicament — in the second poem a fatal one.

In the third group are the poems written by the true cat-lovers. In these we find appreciation of the universal beauty and grace of the feline race, and understanding of cat nature in all its subtle, inconsistent, and capricious charm. To this class belong the elegiac poems by writers who loved their cats as friends, and whose cats undoubtedly loved them in return. John Jortin, in his Latin poem " Epitaphium Felis," one of the most touching memorials to a cat ever penned, testifies to the affection and faithfulness of his pet—as does Joachim du Bellay in his " Epitaphe d'un Chat." Du Bellay—second only to Ronsard in the famous French Renaissance Pléiade group—mourns, with the sensitive apprehension of true grief, his little grey playfellow Belaud, in a poem pervaded throughout by the characteristically poignant and intimate charm which makes this poet so easy to understand and appreciate at a distance of four hundred years.

Another, much later French poet, Charles Baudelaire, wrote of cats with a passion which touched adoration, and a perception which stressed their more esoteric and intuitive qualities. Théophile Gautier writes of him and his cats thus:

They stray about the house with velvety tread, like the *genius loci*; or sit beside the writer's table companioning his thought, gazing at him from the depths of their golden eyes, with intelligent tenderness and intuitive penetration. . . . Their caresses are gentle, delicate, silent, and feminine, and have nothing in common with the noisy, overblown barking and lickings of dogs, who nevertheless attract to themselves all the affection of the common herd.

Gautier, himself an ardent devotee, cannot resist praising his favourites to the detriment of dogs. It is indeed rare to find a human being who does not take sides in this perennial controversy! Elsewhere he tells an amusing story of one of his own cats who, on beholding a parrot for the first time, said, " This is decidedly—yes, it is—a green chicken! "

I am glad to be able to include Baudelaire's famous poem " Les Chats " in Mr MacColl's translation. In another delightful poem to a cat he says:

> C'est l'esprit familier du lieu,
> Il juge, il préside, il inspire.
> Toutes choses dans son empire.
> — Peut-être — est-il fée — est-il dieu?

" Perchance he's a fairy? " In how many myths and fairy-tales he appears. In the earliest of all myths we find the image of the cat moon eating up the grey mice of twilight. The goddess Freya, the Scandinavian Diana, is sometimes depicted in a chariot drawn by a team of cats. Undoubtedly this association of the cat with the moon goddess, who under her other name of Hecate presided over all sorcery, spells, and magic, gave rise to all the legends of cats being witches in disguise, or the familiars of witches.

And then the fairy-tales. Sagacity would seem to be the quality most emphasized in *Puss-in-boots* and *Dick Whittington and his Cat*. The strangest of all is *Knurre Murre*, from which I cannot resist quoting:

> A farmer of Staindrop, in Durham, was one night crossing a bridge when a cat jumped out, stood before him, and, looking him full in the face, said:

"Johnny Reed, Johnny Reed!
Tell Madam Momfort
That Mally Dixon's dead."

The farmer returned home, and in mickle wonder recited this awful stanza to his wife, when up started their black cat, saying, " Is she ? " and disappeared for ever. It was supposed she was a fairy in disguise, who thus went to attend a sister's funeral. . . .

Among the countless legendary anecdotes, two of the most charming are the following. The first of these, which is mentioned by Sir Edmund Gosse, in his essay on cats, refers to " the Prophet Mahomet, who, being consulted one day on a point of piety, preferred to cut off his sleeve on which his favourite pussy was asleep, rather than wake her violently by rising." The second, a most winning story, relates to the Malayan cats, who possess the distinguishing characteristic of knots in their tails, in some cases nearer the body, in others closer to the tip, but always there. The legend goes that whenever a princess of Malaya went to the seashore to bathe she took her favourite cat; and, before she entered the sea, slipped off her rings and slid them on the cat's tail for safety, securing them by a knot. Hence it is that to this day Malayan cats bear the mark of Keeper of the Royal Jewels.

Apart from legends, much prose literature has been devoted to cats. Bartholomew Glanvil, in *De Rerum Natura*, translated by Trevisa in 1398, thus describes the Old English cat:

> The catte is a beaste of uncertain heare and colour, for some catte is white, some rede, some black, some spewed [piebald] and speckled in the fete and in the face and in the eares. And he is . . . in youth swyfte plyante and mery, and lepeth and reseth [rusheth] on all thynge that is tofore him; and is led by a strawe and playeth therwith. And is a right hevy beast in age, and ful slepy, and lieth slily in wait for myce . . . and when he taketh a mous he playeth therwith, and eateth him, after the play. . . . And he maketh a ruthefull noyse and gustful when one proffereth to fyghte with another.

From Hakluyt's *Voyages* (1589) comes the following vivid and delightful anecdote:

It chanced by fortune that the Shippes Cat lept into the sea, which being downe kept herselfe very valiauntly above water, notwithstanding the great waves; still swimming, the which the Master knowing, he caused the skiffe with half a dozen men to goe towards her and fetch her againe, when she was almost half a mile from the Shippe, and all this while the shippe lay on staies. I hardly believe they would have made such haste and meanes, if one of the company had been in like perill. They made the more haste because it was the patron's cat.

Montaigne, playing with his cat, complained that " she thought him but an ass." Many sensitive cat-owners have felt the same misgivings.

Augustin Paradis de Moncrif, in his famous cat book *Les Chats*, published at Rotterdam in 1727, writes of the cats of many distinguished people, especially of those owned by the *précieuses* of the seventeenth century, including the Duchess of Maine and the Duchess of Lésdiguière, who when her pet died erected a mausoleum with a large cat sculptured in marble, set in a grove of poplars. Both Richelieu and Colbert delighted in cats' company, and Pope Gregory the Great made his cat a cardinal. When Henry Wriothesley, Earl of Southampton, Shakespeare's patron, was sent to the Tower of London for treason, his cat found him out by climbing down the chimney, and was his solace in prison.

Dr Samuel Johnson had a cat called Hodge to whom he was much attached. Boswell says:

I never shall forget the indulgence with which he treated Hodge, his cat; for whom he himself used to go out and buy oysters, lest the servants having that trouble, should take a dislike to the poor creature. . . . I recollect him one day scrambling up Dr Johnson's breast, apparently with much satisfaction, while my friend, smiling and half whistling, rubbed down his back, and pulled him by the tail, and when I observed he was a fine cat, saying, " Why, yes, Sir, but I have had cats whom I liked better than this," and then, as if perceiving Hodge to be out of countenance, adding, " but he is a very fine cat, a very fine cat indeed."

That William Cowper, though not over-sympathetic to his " Retired Cat," shut by accident in a chest of drawers, succumbed wholeheartedly to a kitten's irresistible fascination, is shown by the following extract from a letter to his cousin, Lady Hesketh:

> In point of size she is likely to be a kitten always, being extremely small for her age, but time, I suppose, that spoils everything will make her also a cat. You will see her, I hope, before that melancholy period will arrive, for no wisdom that she may gain by experience and reflection, hereafter, will compensate the loss of her present hilarity. She is dressed in a tortoiseshell suit, and I know that you will delight in her.

Sir Richard Steele, writing in *The Tatler*, said that his first actions on arriving home at night were to stir the fire and stroke his cat. Charles Dickens had a kitten called William, who, to attract his attention, taught itself to put out the candle by which its master was reading. Samuel Butler, of *Erewhon* fame, seems to have had two sympathetic ruling passions—Handel's music and cats—and there are many references to these in his *Notebooks* and letters.

In recent years there have been many stories, and even novels, written about cats, and one comprehensive treatise, *The Tiger in the House*, by the American author Carl van Vechten, which deals in the most scholarly and entertaining fashion with the cat, not only in literature, but in all the other arts. Two French writers, " Colette " and Jean Giraudoux, in their respective novels, *Saha* and *Rrou*, show great understanding of, and sympathy with, cat nature. The latter book is a moving tale of a cat's passion for its home, and the long, desperate journey he made to return to it. Eleanor Farjeon has written a delightful book called *Golden Coney*, which relates the history of a family of the well-known Hampstead strain of orange tabbies. Michael Joseph has collected a number of cat stories with the title of *Puss in Books*, and written exquisitely of his Siamese in *Charles: the Story of a Friendship*.

" Saki " (H. H. Munro) wrote a witty story about a cat called Tobermory, surely a descendant of the Cheshire Cat, who broke up a house-party in disorder, by suddenly acquiring human speech and giving away the guests' most shady secrets. In an essay called *The Achievement of the Cat* this author says: "It is indeed no small achievement to have combined the untrammelled liberty of primeval savagery with the luxury which only highly developed civilization can command." In this lies one of the chief fascinations of the cat for his admirers. Self-reliance, courage, and self-respect are characteristics possessed by the feline race down to the smallest kitten. They are also supreme individualists; you could never turn a cat into a Fascist.

The French poet Jules Lemaître said:

> . . . Je salue en toi, calme penseur,
> Deux exquises vertus: scepticisme et douceur.

Scepticism and gentleness—a rare harmony of qualities indeed, and one beloved by poets whether found in human beings or cats.

But it is above all for their beauty and grace, soft as velvet, taut as steel, that we admire these miniature lions and tigers. Who that has ever loved a cat can forget the countless moments of visual delight in his company? One remembers the angel-faced kitten prancing on the grass sideways, with tiny tail stuck straight up; the leggy adolescent, full of intelligent curiosity when confronted with hedgehog or spider; a little black cat in his prime, glossy as a seal, moving through a bed of flame-coloured snapdragons on a summer morning, his eyes shining like wet jade in the sunshine; and the same cat jumping with ecstatic witch leaps in the moonlight. But it is not suitable for the mere editor to let "unfetter'd Fancy fly." I leave that to the poets who follow, with the hope that readers will find, as I have, that scarcely any aspect of the subject—even the mystical, as in Christopher Smart's strangely appealing poem—has been neglected.

For the Cherub Cat is a term of the Angel Tiger.

THE CAT AND THE PARTRIDGE

YOUR master grieved as though you'd savaged *him*,
When you devoured his partridge, wicked cat.
The hounds which tore Actæon limb from limb,
Fierce man-eaters, did hardly worse than that.
And now so set on partridge is your soul,
The mice can dance and rob your dainty bowl.

>   DAMOCHARIS THE GRAMMARIAN (*c. A.D. 550*)
>   "*Anthologia Palatina*," Book VII, *No.* 206
>   *translated from the Greek by W. Bedell Stanford*

PANGUR BÁN

I AND Pangur Bán, my cat,
'Tis a like task we are at;
Hunting mice is his delight,
Hunting words I sit all night.

Better far than praise of men
'Tis to sit with book and pen;
Pangur bears me no ill-will,
He too plies his simple skill.

'Tis a merry thing to see
At our tasks how glad are we,
When at home we sit and find
Entertainment to our mind.

Oftentimes a mouse will stray
In the hero Pangur's way;
Oftentimes my keen thought set
Takes a meaning in its net.

'Gainst the wall he sets his eye
Full and fierce, and sharp and sly;
'Gainst the wall of knowledge I
All my little wisdom try.

When a mouse darts from its den,
O how glad is Pangur then!
O what gladness do I prove
When I solve the doubts I love!

So in peace our tasks we ply,
Pangur Bán, my cat, and I;
In our arts we find our bliss,
I have mine and he has his.

Practice every day has made
Pangur perfect in his trade;
I get wisdom day and night,
Turning darkness into light.

ANONYMOUS (eighth century)
translated from the Irish by Dr Robin Flower

HUNGRY MASTER AND HUNGRY CAT

WHEN my house was bare of skins and pots of meal,
after it had been inhabited, not empty, full of folk and richly
    prosperous,
I see the mice avoid my house, retiring to the governor's palace.
The flies have called for a move, whether their wings are
    clipped or whole.
The cat stayed a year in the house and did not see a mouse
shaking its head at hunger, at a life full of pain and spite.
When I saw the pained downcast head, the heat in the belly, I
    said,
"Patience; you are the best cat my eyes ever saw in a ward."
He said, "I have no patience. How can I stay in a desert like
    the belly of a she ass?"
I said, "Go in peace to a hotel where travellers are many and
    much trade,
Even if the spider spins in my wine jar, in the jug, and the pot."

ABU SHAMAQMAQ (c. A.D. 770)
translated from the Arabic by Dr A. S. Tritton

TO A CAT

Poor Puss is gone! 'Tis fate's decree—
Yet I must still her loss deplore,
For dearer than a child was she,
And ne'er shall I behold her more.

With many a sad presaging tear
This morn I saw her steal away,
While she went on without a fear
Except that she should miss her prey.

I saw her to the dove-house climb,
With cautious feet and slow she stept,
Resolved to balance loss of time
By eating faster than she crept.

Her subtle foes were on the watch
And mark'd her course, with fury fraught,
And while she hoped the birds to catch,
An arrow's point the huntress caught.

In fancy she had got them all,
And drunk their blood, and suck'd their breath;
Alas! she only got a fall,
And only drank the draught of death.

Why, why was pigeons' flesh so nice,
That thoughtless cats should love it thus?
Hadst thou but lived on rats and mice,
Thou hadst been living still, poor Puss.

Curst be the taste, howe'er refined,
That prompts us for such joys to wish,
And curst the dainty where we find
Destruction lurking in the dish.

Ibn Alalaf Alnaharwany (*A.D. 829*)
translated from the Arabic by J. D. Carlyle

EPITAPH ON A PET CAT

My life seems dull and flat,
And, as you'll wonder what,
Magny, has made this so,
I want you first to know
It's not for rings or purse
But something so much worse:
Three days ago I lost
All that I value most,
My treasure, my delight;
I cannot speak, or write,
Or even think of what
Belaud, my small grey cat,
Meant to me, tiny creature,
Masterpiece of nature
In the whole world of cats—
And certain death to rats!—
Whose beauty was worthy
Of immortality.

Belaud, first let me say,
Was not entirely grey
Like cats bred here at home,
But more like those in Rome,
His fur being silver-grey
And fine and smooth as satin,
While, lying back, he'd display
A white expanse of ermine.

Small muzzle, tiny teeth;
Eyes of a tempered warmth,
Whose pupils of dark-green
Showed every colour seen
In the bow which splendidly
Arches the rainy sky.

Plump neck, short ears, height
To his head proportionate;
Beneath his ebony nostrils
His little leonine muzzle's
Prim beauty, which appeared
Fringed by the silvery beard
Which gave such waggish grace
To his young dandy's face.

His slender leg, small foot—
No lambswool scarf could be
More soft, except when he
Unsheathed and scratched with it!
His neat and downy throat,
Long monkey's tail, and coat
Diversely flecked and freckled,
In natural motley speckled;
His flank and round stomach
Under control, his back
Longish—a Syrian
If ever there was one!

This was Belaud, a gentle
Animal, whose title
To beauty was so sure
He'd no competitor!
A sad and bitter cross!
Irreparable loss!
It almost seems to me
That Death, though he must be
More ruthless than a bear,
Would, if he'd known my rare
Belaud, have felt his heart
Soften—and for my part
I would not wince and shrink
So from life's joys, I think.

But Death has never watched
Him as he jumped or scratched,
Laughed at his nimble tricks,
His many wild frolics,
Admired the sprightly grace
With which he'd turn, or race,
Or, with one whirl of cat,
Tumble, or seize a rat
And play with it—and then
Would make me laugh again
By rubbing at his jaw
With such a frisky paw
In such a dashing manner!
Or when the little monster
Leapt quietly on my bed,
Or when he took his bread
Or meat most daintily
Straight from my lips—for he
Showed in such various ways
His quaint, engaging traits!

What fun to watch him dance,
Scamper, and skate, and prance
After a ball of thread;
To see his silly head
Whirl like a spinning wheel
After his velvet tail;
Or, when he made of it
A girdle, and would sit
Solemnly on the ground,
Showing his fluffy round
Of paunch, seeming to be
Learned in theology,
The spit of some well-known
Doctor at the Sorbonne!
And how, when he was teased,
He used to fence with us—

Yet if we stopped to fuss
Was very soon appeased!

O Magny, now you see
How he diverted me,
You'll realize why I mourn—
And surely no cat born
Has ever had so nice
A style with rats and mice!

He would come unawares
Upon them in their lairs,
And not one could escape
Unless he'd thought to scrape
A second hole—no rat
Ever outran that cat!
And let me add at once
My Belaud was no dunce,
But very teachable,
Knowing how to eat at table—
When offered food, that is:
That eager paw you'd see,
Held out so flirtingly,
Might scratch you otherwise!

Belaud was well-behaved
And in no way depraved;
His only ravages
Were on an ancient cheese,
A finch, and a young linnet
Whose trillings seemed to get
On Belaud's nerves—but then
How perfect are we men?

He wasn't the sort to be
Out everlastingly
After more food to eat,
But was content to wait

Until his meals, when he
Ate without gluttony.

Also he was by nature
A well-conducted creature;
For he would never spread
His traces far and wide
Like many cats, but tried
To live as a well-bred
Feline should live and be
In all his ways cleanly . . .

He was my favourite plaything;
And not for ever purring
A long and tunelessly
Grumbling litany,
But kept in his complainings
To kitten-like miaowings.

My only memory
Of him annoying me
Is that, sometimes at night
When rats began to gnaw
And rustle in my straw
Mattress, he'd waken me
Seizing most dexterously
Upon them in their flight.

Now that the cruel right hand
Of Death comes to demand
My bodyguard from me,
My sweet security
Gives way to hideous fears;
Rats come and gnaw my ears,
And mice and rats at night
Chew up the lines I write!

The gods have sympathy
For poor humanity;

An animal's death foretells
Some evil that befalls,
For heaven can speak by these
And other presages.
The day fate cruelly
Took my small dog from me—
My Peloton—the sense
Of evil influence
Filled me with utter dread;
And then I lost my cat:
What crueller storm than that
Could break upon my head!

He was my very dear
Companion everywhere,
My room, my bed, my table,
Even more companionable
Than a little dog; for he
Was never one of those
Monsters that hideously
Fill night with their miaows;
And now he can't become,
Poor little puss, a tom—
Sad loss, by which his splendid
Line is abruptly ended.

God grant to me, Belaud,
Command of speech to show
Your gentle nature forth
In words of fitting worth,
Your qualities to state
In verse as delicate,
That you may live while cats
Wage mortal war on rats.

JOACHIM DU BELLAY (*1525-60*)
translated from the French by R. N. Currey

THE LOVER, WHOSE MISTRESSE FEARED A MOUSE, DECLARETH THAT HE WOULD BECOME A CAT IF HE MIGHT HAVE HIS DESIRE

If I might alter kind,
   What, think you, I would be?
Not Fish, nor Foule, nor Fle, nor Frog,
   Nor Squirrel on the Tree;
The Fish, the Hooke, the Foule
   The lymèd Twig doth catch,
The Fle, the Finger, and the Frog
   The Bustard doth dispatch.

The Squirrel thinking nought,
   That feately cracks the nut;
The greedie Goshawke wanting prey,
   In dread of Death doth put;
But scorning all these kindes,
   I would become a Cat,
To combat with the creeping Mouse,
   And scratch the screeking Rat.

I would be present, aye,
   And at my Ladie's call,
To gard her from the fearfull Mouse,
   In Parlour and in Hall;
In Kitchen, for his Lyfe,
   He should not shew his hed;
The Pease in Poke should lie untoucht
   When shee were gone to Bed.

The Mouse should stand in Feare,
   So should the squeaking Rat;
All this would I doe if I were
   Converted to a Cat.

GEORGE TURBERVILLE (*1540?–1610*)

EPITAPH ON THE DUCHESS OF MAINE'S CAT

Puss passer-by, within this simple tomb
Lies one whose life fell Atropos hath shred;
The happiest cat on earth hath heard her doom,
And sleeps for ever in a marble bed.
Alas! what long delicious days I've seen!
O cats of Egypt, my illustrious sires,
You who on altars, bound with garlands green,
Have melted hearts, and kindled fond desires,
Hymns in your praise were paid, and offerings too,
But I'm not jealous of those rights divine,
Since Ludovisa loved me, close and true,
Your ancient glory was less proud than mine.
To live a simple pussy by her side
Was nobler far than to be deified.

LA MOTHE LE VAYER (*1588–1672*)
translated from the French by Sir Edmund Gosse

CAT INTO LADY

A MAN possessed a Cat on which he doted.
So fine she was, so soft, so silky-coated—
Her very mew had quality!
He was as mad as mad could be.
So one fine day by dint of supplications,
And tears, and charms, and conjurations,
He worked upon the Powers above
To turn her woman; and the loon
Took her to wife that very afternoon.
Before, 'twas fondness crazed him: now 'twas love!
Never did peerless beauty fire
Her suitor with more wild desire
Than this unprecedented spouse
Th' eccentric partner of his vows.
They spend their hours in mutual coaxing,

He sees each day less trace of cat,
And lastly, hoaxed beyond all hoaxing,
Deems her sheer woman through and through;
Till certain mice, who came to gnaw the mat,
Disturbed the couple at their bill-and-coo.
The wife leapt up—but missed her chance;
And soon, their fears allayed by her new guise,
The mice crept back: this time she was in stance,
And took 'em by surprise.
Thenceforth all means were unavailing
T'eradicate her little failing.

The bent we are born with rules us till we die.
It laughs at schooling: by a certain age
The vessel smacks, the stuff has ta'en its ply.
Man strives in vain to disengage
His will from this necessity.
Our nature, so confirmed by use,
Binds us in chains that none may loose:
Whips and scorpions, brands and burns,
Leave it as it was before:
If you drive it through the door,
By the window it returns.

JEAN DE LA FONTAINE (*1621–95*)
translated from the French by Sir Edward Marsh

THE CAT AND THE FOX

WITH pious mien, a Fox and a Tom-cat,
Each with his pilgrim staff and hat,
Set out together on their way,
And as they went they seemed to pray;
Though a more precious pair of rank impostors
Never intoned their Paternosters.
For their expenses they recouped themselves
With spoil from hen-roosts and from dairy-shelves;

And when the road seemed long and drear,
An argument restored their cheer—
(Discussion is the thing, to keep
Oneself from dropping off to sleep!).
They talked philosophy till all was blue,
Then scandal: that exhausted too,
The Fox began: " You claim to be so clever—
Can you beat me? My bag holds tricks in scores."
" No," said the Cat, " I stick to one: however,
'Tis worth a thousand such as yours."
Hammer-and tongs the clack breaks out anew,
Till hark, near by, the view-halloo!
" Now for your bag," says Tabby, " now to rack
For some sure ruse that crafty brain.
Here's mine, 'tis good enough for me."
Therewith he bounded up a tree.
The other starts to dodge and veer and tack,
Here, there, and everywhere, and back,
Bolts down a hundred holes and out again,
Contrives for many an anxious hour to strain
The whole resources of the veteran pack.
Alas, 'twas all in vain!
Smoke, and the terriers, played their mutual rôle;
And when he popt his head from the last hole
The game was up: an ambushed hound
Was on him at a single bound.

To have too many plans is a delusion:
It tends to vacillation and confusion;
So have one only, but be sure 'tis sound.

JEAN DE LA FONTAINE
translated from the French by Sir Edward Marsh

TO MY LORD BUCKHURST, VERY YOUNG, PLAYING WITH A CAT

The am'rous Youth, whose tender Breast
Was by his darling Cat possest,
Obtain'd of Venus his Desire,
Howe'er irregular his Fire:
Nature the Pow'r of Love obey'd:
The Cat became a blushing Maid;
And, on the happy Change, the Boy
Imploy'd his Wonder and his Joy.

   Take care, O beauteous Child, take care,
Lest Thou prefer so rash a Pray'r:
Nor vainly hope, the Queen of Love
Will e'er thy Fav'rite's Charms improve.
O quickly from her Shrine retreat;
Or tremble for thy Darling's Fate.

   The Queen of Love, who soon will see
Her own Adonis live in Thee,
Will lightly her first Loss deplore;
Will easily forgive the Boar:
Her Eyes with Tears no more will flow;
With jealous Rage her Breast will glow:
And on her tabby Rival's Face
She deep will mark her new Disgrace.

                        Matthew Prior (*1664–1721*)

UPON A FRIEND'S PET CAT, BEING SICK

How fickle's Health! when sickness thus
So sharp, so sudden visits *Puss*!
A warning fair, and Instance good,
To show how frail are Flesh and Blood,
That Fate has Mortals at a Call,
Men, Women, Children—Cats and all.

Nor should we fear, despair, or sorrow,
If well to-day, and ill to-morrow,
Grief being but a Med'cine vain,
For griping Gut, or aking Brain,
And Patience the best Cure for Pain.
How brisk and well, last Week, was *Puss*!
How sleek, and plump, as one of us:
Yet now, alack! and well-a-day!
How dull, how rough, and fall'n away.
How feintly creeps about the House!
Regardless or of Play, or Mouse;
Nor stomach has, to drink, or eat,
Of sweetest Milk, or daintiest Meat;
A grievous this, and sore Disaster
To all the House, but most his Master,
Who sadly takes it thus to heart,
As in his Pains he bore a part.
And, what increases yet his Grief,
Is, nought can cure, or give Relief,
No Doctor caring to prescribe,
Or Med'cine give, for Love, or Bribe,
Nor other Course, but to petition
Dame Nature, oft the best Physician,
The readiest too, and cheapest sure,
Since she ne'er asks a Fee for Cure
Nor ever takes a single Shilling,
As many basely do for killing.
So, for a while, snug let him lye,
As Fates decree, to live or dye,
While I, in dismal dogrel Verse,
His Beauties and his Fame rehearse.
Poor *Bob*! how have I smiled to see
Thee sitting on thy Master's Knee?
While, pleased to stroke thy Tabby-coat,
Sweet Purrings warbling in thy Throat,
He would with rapturous Hug declare,
No Voice more sweet, or Maid more fair.

No prating Poll, or Monkey bold,
Was more caress'd by Woman old,
Nor flutt'ring Fop, with Am'rous Tongue,
So much admir'd by Virgin Young.
Miss *Betty's* Bed-fellow, and Pet,
(Too young to have another yet),
At Dinner, he'd beside her sit,
Fed from her Mouth with sweetest Bit;
Not Mrs L——'s so charming *Philly*
Was more familiar, fond, or silly,
Nor Mrs C——'s ugly Cur
Made more a foustre, or more stir.
Oft tir'd, and cloy'd, with being petted,
Or else by *Molly* beaten, fretted,
He'd out into the Garden run,
To sleep in th' Shade, or bask in th' Sun;
Sometimes about the Walks he'd ramble,
Or on the verdant Green would amble,
Or under the hedges sculking sit,
To catch the unwary *Wren*, or *Tit*,
Or *Sparrows* young, which Sun-beams hot
Had forc'd to quit their mansion Pot,
Then murther with relentless Claws.
Now, cruel Death, so fierce and grim,
With gaping jaws does threaten him,
While pining, he, with Sickness sore,
Oppress'd and griev'd, can hunt no more.

Now joyful Mice skip, frisk, and play,
And safely revel, Night and Day.
The Garrets, Kitchens, Stairs, and Entry,
Unguarded by that dreadful Centry.

The Pantry now is open set,
No fear for *Puss* therein to get,
With Chicken cold to run away,
Or sip the Cream set by for Tea;

Jenny now need not watch the Door,
Or for lost Meat repine no more,
Nor *Molly* many a scolding dread
For slamming him from off the Bed;
Poor harmless Animal! now lies
As who can say, he lives or dies.
Tho' I have heard a saying that
Some three times three Lives has a Cat;
Should Death then now the Conquest gain,
And feeble *Bob*, with struggle vain,
To his resistless Fate give way,
Yet come to Life, another Day,
How will Time scratch his old bald Pate,
To see himself so *Bobb'd*, so Bit,
To find that *Bob* has eight Lives more
To lose, e'er he can him secure.
Should he however, this Bout dye,
What Pen should write his Elegy?
No living Bard is fit, not One;
Since *Addison*, and Parnel's gone;
Or such another Pen, as that
Which wrote so fine on Mountaign's Cat.

    JOHN WINSTANLEY (*1678–1751*)

THE RAT-CATCHER AND CATS

THE rats by night such mischief did,
Betty was every morning chid.
They undermined whole sides of bacon,
Her cheese was sapp'd, her tarts were taken,
Her pasties fenced with thickest paste,
Were all demolish'd, and laid waste.
She cursed the Cat for want of duty,
Who left her foes a constant booty.
 An engineer, of noted skill,
Engaged to stop the growing ill.

    From room to room he now surveys
Their haunts, their works, their secret ways;
Finds where they 'scape and ambuscade,
And whence the nightly sally's made,
    An envious Cat, from place to place,
Unseen attends his silent pace.
She saw that if his trade went on,
The purring race must be undone;
So, secretly removes his baits,
And ev'ry stratagem defeats.
    Again he sets the poison'd toils,
And Puss again the labour foils.
    What foe (to frustrate my designs)
My schemes thus nightly countermines?
Incensed, he cries, this very hour
The wretch shall bleed beneath my power.
    So said, a pond'rous trap he brought,
And in the fact poor Puss was caught.
    Smuggler, says he, thou shalt be made
A victim to our loss of trade.
    The captive Cat, with piteous mews,
For pardon, life, and freedom sues.
A sister of the science spare;
One int'rest is our common care.
    What insolence! the man replied;
Shall cats with us the game divide?
Were all your interloping band
Extinguish'd or expell'd the land,
We Rat-catchers might raise our fees,
Sole guardians of a nation's cheese!
    A Cat, who saw the lifted knife,
Thus spoke, and saved her sister's life:
    In ev'ry age and clime we see,
Two of a trade can ne'er agree.
Each hates his neighbour for encroaching;
'Squire stigmatizes 'squire for poaching;
Beauties with beauties are in arms,

And scandal pelts each other's charms;
Kings, too, their neighbour kings dethrone,
In hope to make the world their own,
But let us limit our desires,
Not war like beauties, kings, and 'squires!
For though we both one prey pursue,
There's game enough for us and you.

JOHN GAY (*1685–1732*)

LISY'S PARTING WITH HER CAT

THE dreadful hour with leaden pace approached,
Lashed fiercely on by unrelenting fate,
When Lisy and her bosom Cat must part:
For now, to school and pensive needle doomed,
She's banished from her childhood's undashed joy,
And all the pleasing intercourse she kept
With her grey comrade, which has often soothed
Her tender moments while the world around
Glowed with ambition, business, and vice,
Or lay dissolved in sleep's delicious arms;
And from their dewy orbs the conscious stars
Shed on their friendship influence benign.
 But see where mournful Puss, advancing, stood
With outstretched tail, casts looks of anxious woe
On melting Lisy, in whose eyes the tear
Stood tremulous, and thus would fain have said,
If Nature had not tied her struggling tongue:
"Unkind, O! who shall now with fattening milk,
With flesh, with bread, and fish beloved, and meat,
Regale my taste? and at the cheerful fire,
Ah, who shall bask me in their downy lap?
Who shall invite me to the bed, and throw
The bedclothes o'er me in the winter night,
When Eurus roars? Beneath whose soothing hand

Soft shall I purr? But now, when Lisy's gone,
What is the dull officious world to me?
I loathe the thoughts of life: " Thus plained the cat,
While Lisy felt, by sympathetic touch,
These anxious thoughts that in her mind revolved,
And casting on her a desponding look,
She snatched her in her arms with eager grief,
And mewing, thus began: " O Cat beloved!
Thou dear companion of my tender years!
Joy of my youth! that oft has licked my hands
With velvet tongue ne'er stained by mouse's blood.
Oh, gentle Cat! how shall I part with thee?
How dead and heavy will the moments pass
When you are not in my delighted eye,
With Cubi playing, or your flying tail.
How harshly will the softest muslin feel,
And all the silk of schools, while I no more
Have your sleek skin to soothe my softened sense?
How shall I eat while you are not beside
To share the bit? How shall I ever sleep
While I no more your lulling murmurs hear?
Yet we must part—so rigid fate decrees—
But never shall your loved idea dear
Part from my soul, and when I first can mark
The embroidered figure on the snowy lawn,
Your image shall my needle keen employ.
Hark! now I'm called away! O direful sound!
I come—I come, but first I charge you all—
You—you—and you, particularly you,
O, Mary, Mary, feed her with the best,
Repose her nightly in the warmest couch,
And be a Lisy to her! "—Having said,
She set her down, and with her head across,
Rushed to the evil which she could not shun,
While a sad mew went knelling to her heart!

      JAMES THOMSON (*1700–48*)

ON THE DEATH OF A FAVOURITE CAT, DROWNED IN A TUB OF GOLD FISHES

'Twas on a lofty vase's side,
Where China's gayest art had dy'd
   The azure flowers that blow;
Demurest of the tabby kind,
The pensive Selima, reclin'd,
   Gaz'd on the lake below.

Her conscious tail her joy declar'd;
The fair round face, the snowy beard,
   The velvet of her paws,
Her coat, that with the tortoise vies,
Her ears of jet, and emerald eyes,
   She saw; and purr'd applause.

Still had she gaz'd; but 'midst the tide
Two angel forms were seen to glide,
   The Genii of the stream:
Their scaly armour's Tyrian hue
Thro' richest purple to the view
   Betray'd a golden gleam.

The hapless Nymph with wonder saw:
A whisker first, and then a claw,
   With many an ardent wish,
She stretch'd in vain to reach the prize.
What female heart can gold despise?
   What Cat's averse to fish?

Presumptuous Maid! with looks intent
Again she stretch'd, again she bent,
   Nor knew the gulf between.
(Malignant Fate sat by, and smil'd.)
The slipp'ry verge her feet beguil'd,
   She tumbled headlong in.

Eight times emerging from the flood
She mew'd to ev'ry wat'ry God,
   Some speedy aid to send.
No Dolphin came, no Nereid stirr'd:
Nor cruel *Tom*, nor *Susan* heard.
   A Fav'rite has no friend!

From hence, ye Beauties, undeceiv'd,
Know, one false step is ne'er retriev'd,
   And be with caution bold.
Not all that tempts your wand'ring eyes
And heedless hearts, is lawful prize;
   Nor all that glisters, gold.

THOMAS GRAY (*1716–71*)

THE CAT

... For I will consider my Cat Jeoffrey.

For he is the servant of the Living God, duly and daily serving him.

For at the first glance of the glory of God in the East he worships in his way.

For is this done by wreathing his body seven times round with elegant quickness.

For then he leaps up to catch the musk, which is the blessing of God upon his prayer.

For he rolls up on prank to work it in.

For having done duty and received blessing he begins to consider himself.

For this he performs in ten degrees.

For first he looks upon his fore-paws to see if they are clean.

For secondly he kicks up behind to clear a way there.

For thirdly he works it upon stretch with his fore-paws extended.

For fourthly he sharpens his paws by wood.

For fifthly he washes himself.

For sixthly he rolls upon wash.

For seventhly he fleas himself, that he may not be interrupted upon the beat.
For eighthly he rubs himself against a post.
For ninthly he looks up for his instructions.
For tenthly he goes in quest of food.
For having consider'd God and himself he will consider his neighbour.
For if he meets another cat he will kiss her in kindness.
For when he takes his prey he plays with it to give it chance.
For one mouse in seven escapes by his dallying.
For when his day's work is done his business more properly begins.
For he keeps the Lord's watch in the night against the adversary.
For he counteracts the powers of darkness by his electrical skin and glaring eyes.
For he counteracts the Devil, who is death, by brisking about the life.
For in his morning orisons he loves the sun and the sun loves him.
For he is of the tribe of Tiger.
For the Cherub Cat is a term of the Angel Tiger . . .

CHRISTOPHER SMART (*1722–71*)

THE RETIRED CAT

A POET's cat, sedate and grave,
As poet well could wish to have,
Was much addicted to inquire
For nooks to which she might retire,
And where, secure as mouse in chink,
She might repose, or sit and think.
I know not where she caught the trick—
Nature perhaps herself had cast her
In such a mould *philosophique*,
Or else she learned it of her master.

Sometimes ascending, debonair,
An apple-tree or lofty pear,
Lodg'd with convenience in the fork,
She watched the gard'ner at his work;
Sometimes her ease and solace sought
In an old empty wat'ring pot,
There wanting nothing, save a fan,
To seem some nymph in her sedan,
Apparell'd in exactest sort,
And ready to be borne to court.

   But love of change it seems has place
Not only in our wiser race;
Cats also feel as well as we
That passion's force, and so did she.
Her climbing, she began to find,
Expos'd her too much to the wind,
And the old utensil of tin
Was cold and comfortless within:
She therefore wish'd instead of those,
Some place of more serene repose,
Where neither cold might come, nor air
Too rudely wanton with her hair,
And sought it in the likeliest mode
Within her master's snug abode.

   A draw'r—it chanc'd, at bottom lin'd
With linen of the softest kind,
With such as merchants introduce
From India, for the ladies' use—
A draw'r impending o'er the rest,
Half open in the topmost chest,
Of depth enough, and none to spare,
Invited her to slumber there.
Puss, with delight beyond expression,
Survey'd the scene, and took possession.
Recumbent at her ease ere long,
And lulled by her own humdrum song,
She left the cares of life behind,

And slept as she would sleep her last,
When in came, housewifely inclin'd,
The chambermaid, and shut it fast,
By no malignity impell'd,
But all unconscious whom it held.

 Awaken'd by the shock (cried puss)
Was ever cat attended thus!
The open draw'r was left, I see,
Merely to prove a nest for me,
For soon as I was well compos'd,
Then came the maid, and it was closed:
How smooth these 'kerchiefs, and how sweet.
O what a delicate retreat!
I will resign myself to rest
Till Sol, declining in the west,
Shall call to supper; when, no doubt,
Susan will come and let me out.

 The evening came, the sun descended,
And puss remain'd still unattended.
The night roll'd tardily away
(With her indeed 'twas never day),
The sprightly morn her course renew'd,
The evening grey again ensued,
And puss came into mind no more
Than if entomb'd the day before.
With hunger pinch'd, and pinch'd for room,
She now presag'd approaching doom,
Nor slept a single wink, or purr'd,
Conscious of jeopardy incurr'd.

 That night, by chance the poet, watching,
Heard an inexplicable scratching,
His noble heart went pit-a-pat,
And to himself he said—what's that?
He drew the curtain at his side,
And forth he peep'd, but nothing spied.
Yet, by his ear directed, guess'd
Something imprison'd in the chest,

And doubtful what, with prudent care,
Resolv'd it should continue there.
At length a voice, which well he knew,
A long and melancholy mew,
Saluting his poetic ears,
Consol'd him, and dispell'd his fears;
He left his bed, he trod the floor,
He 'gan in haste the draw'rs explore,
The lowest first, and without stop,
The rest in order to the top.
For 'tis a truth well known to most,
That whatsoever thing is lost,
We seek it, ere it come to light,
In ev'ry cranny but the right.
Forth skipp'd the cat; not now replete
As erst with airy self-conceit,
Nor in her own fond apprehension
A theme for all the world's attention,
But modest, sober, cur'd of all
Her notions hyperbolical,
And wishing for a place of rest
Anything rather than a chest:
Then stept the poet into bed,
With this reflexion in his head:

MORAL

Beware of too sublime a sense
Of your own worth and consequence!
The man who dreams himself so great
And his importance of such weight,
That all around, in all that's done,
Must move and act for him alone,
Will learn, in school of tribulation,
The folly of his expectation.

WILLIAM COWPER (*1751–1800*)

THE COLUBRIAD

Close by the threshold of a door nail'd fast
Three kittens sat: each kitten look'd aghast.
I, passing swift and inattentive by,
At the three kittens cast a careless eye;
Not much concern'd to know what they did there,
Not deeming kittens worth a poet's care.
But presently a loud and furious hiss
Caused me to stop, and to exclaim—what's this?
When, lo! upon the threshold met my view,
With head erect, and eyes of fiery hue,
A viper, long as Count de Grasse's queue.
Forth from his head his forkèd tongue he throws,
Darting it full against a kitten's nose;
Who having never seen in field or house
The like, sat still and silent, as a mouse:
Only, projecting with attention due
Her whisker'd face, she ask'd him—who are you?
On to the hall went I, with pace not slow,
But swift as lightning, for a long Dutch hoe;
With which well arm'd I hasten'd to the spot,
To find the viper. But I found him not,
And, turning up the leaves and shrubs around,
Found only, that he was not to be found.
But still the kittens, sitting as before
Sat watching close the bottom of the door.
I hope—said I—the villain I would kill
Has slipt between the door and the door's sill;
And if I make dispatch, and follow hard,
No doubt but I shall find him in the yard—
For long ere now it should have been rehears'd,
'Twas in the garden that I found him first.
E'en there I found him; there the full-grown cat
His head with velvet paw did gently pat,
As curious as the kittens erst had been
To learn what this phenomenon might mean.

Fill'd with heroic ardour at the sight,
And fearing every moment he might bite,
And rob our household of our only cat
That was of age to combat with a rat,
With outstretch'd hoe I slew him at the door,
And taught him NEVER TO COME THERE NO MORE.

WILLIAM COWPER

FAMILIARITY DANGEROUS

As in her ancient mistress' lap,
    The youthful tabby lay,
They gave each other many a tap,
    Alike dispos'd to play.

But strife ensues. Puss waxes warm,
    And with protruded claws
Ploughs all the length of Lydia's arm,
    Mere wantonness the cause.

At once, resentful of the deed,
    She shakes her to the ground
With many a threat, that she shall bleed
    With still a deeper wound.

But, Lydia, bid thy fury rest!
    It was a venial stroke;
For she, that will with kittens jest,
    Should bear a kitten's joke.

WILLIAM COWPER
translated from the Latin of Vincent Bourne

AN ODE TO EIGHT CATS BELONGING TO ISRAEL MENDEZ, A JEW

Scene: *The street in a country town.* Time: *Midnight: the poet at his chamber window*

Singers of Israel, O ye singers sweet,
   Who with your gentle mouths from ear to ear,
Pour forth rich symphonies from street to street,
   And to the sleepless wretch, the night endear!

Lo, in my shirt, on you these eyes I fix,
Admiring much the quaintness of your tricks!
   Your friskings, crawlings, squalls, I much approve;
Your spittings, pawings, high-raised rumps,
Swelled tails and Merry-Andrew's jumps,
   With the wild minstrelsy of rapturous love.

How sweetly roll your gooseberry eyes,
As loud you tune your amorous cries,
   And loving scratch each other black and blue!
No boys in wantonness now bang your backs,
No curs, no fiercer mastiffs, tear your flax,
   But all the moonlight world seems made for you.

[*Three verses omitted*]

Good gods! Ye sweet love-chanting rams!
How nimble are you with your hams
   To mount a house, to scale a chimney-top,
And peeping from that chimney-hole,
Pour in a doleful cry, the impassioned soul,
   Inviting Miss Grimalkin to come up:

Who, sweet obliging female, far from coy,
Answers your invitation note with joy,
   And scorning 'midst the ashes more to mope;

Lo! borne on Love's all-daring wing
She mounteth with a pickle-herring spring,
   Without the assistance of a rope.

Dear mousing tribe, my limbs are waxing cold—
   Singers of Israel sweet, adieu, adieu!
I don't suppose you need now to be told
   How much I wish that I was one of you.

        "PETER PINDAR" (JOHN WOLCOT) (*1738–1819*)

EPITAPHIUM FELIS

BY weight of the wearying years, and by grievous illness
Compelled, I come at last to the Lethean lake-side;
"Have thou Elysian suns," said Proserpina, smiling, "Elysian
   meadows."
Nay, but if I deserve it, O kindly Queen of the silence,
Grant me this boon, one night to return to the homestead,
Home to return by night, and into the master's ear,
Whisper, "Across the waste of the Stygian waters
Your Felis, most faithful of cats, still holds you dear."

        JOHN JORTIN (*1756*)
        translated from the Latin by Seumas O'Sullivan

THE KITTEN

WANTON droll, whose harmless play
Beguiles the rustic's closing day,
When, drawn the evening fire about,
Sit aged crone and thoughtless lout,
And child upon his three-foot stool,
Waiting until his supper cool,
And maid, whose cheek outblooms the rose,
As bright the blazing faggot glows,

Who bending to the friendly light,
Plies her task with busy sleight;
Come, show thy tricks and sportive graces,
Thus circled round with merry faces!

Backward coil'd and crouching low,
With glaring eyeballs watch thy foe,
The housewife's spindle whirling round,
Or thread, or straw, that on the ground
Its shadow throws, by urchin sly
Held out to lure thy roving eye;
Then stealing onward, fiercely spring
Upon the tempting, faithless thing.
Now, whirling round with bootless skill,
Thy bo-peep tail provokes thee still,
As still beyond thy curving side
Its jetty tip is seen to glide;
Till from thy centre starting far,
Thou sidelong veer'st with rump in air
Erected stiff, and gait awry,
Like madam in her tantrums high;
Though ne'er a madam of them all,
Whose silken kirtle sweeps the hall,
More varied trick and whim displays
To catch the admiring stranger's gaze.

Doth power in measured verses dwell,
All thy vagaries wild to tell?
Ah no! the start, the jet, the bound,
The giddy scamper round and round,
With leap and toss and high curvet,
And many a whirling somerset
(Permitted by the modern Muse
Expression technical to use),
These mock the deftest rhymester's skill,
But poor in art, though rich in will.
The featest tumbler, stage bedight,
To thee is but a clumsy wight,

Who every limb and sinew strains
To do what costs thee little pains;
For which, I trow, the gaping crowd
Requites him oft with plaudits loud.
But, stopp'd the while thy wanton play,
Applauses too thy pains repay:
For then beneath some urchin's hand
With modest pride thou tak'st thy stand,
While many a stroke of kindness glides
Along thy back and tabby sides.
Dilated swells thy glossy fur,
And loudly croons thy busy purr,
As, timing well the equal sound,
Thy clutching feet bepat the ground,
And all their harmless claws disclose
Like prickles of an early rose,
While softly from thy whisker'd cheek
Thy half-closed eyes peer, mild and meek.

But not alone by cottage fire
Do rustics rude thy feats admire.
The learned sage, whose thoughts explore
The widest range of human lore,
Or with unfetter'd fancy fly
Through airy heights of poesy,
Pausing, smiles with alter'd air
To see thee climb his elbow-chair,
Or, struggling on the mat below,
Hold warfare with his slipper'd toe.
The widow'd dame, or lonely maid,
Who, in the still, but cheerless shade
Of home unsocial, spends her age,
And rarely turns a letter'd page,
Upon her hearth for thee lets fall
The rounded cork, or paper ball,
Nor chides thee on thy wicked watch,
The ends of ravell'd skein to catch,

But lets thee have thy wayward will,
Perplexing oft her better skill.

E'en he, whose mind of gloomy bent,
In lonely tower, or prison pent,
Reviews the coil of former days,
And loathes the world and all its ways;
What time the lamp's unsteady gleam
Hath roused him from his moody dream,
Feels, as thou gambol'st round his seat,
His heart of pride less fiercely beat,
And smiles, a link in thee to find,
That joins it still to living kind.

Whence hast thou then, thou witless puss,
The magic power to charm us thus?
Is it that in thy glaring eye
And rapid movements, we descry—
Whilst we at ease, secure from ill,
The chimney corner snugly fill—
A lion darting on his prey,
A tiger at his ruthless play?
Or, is it, that in thee we trace
With all thy varied wanton grace,
An emblem, view'd with kindred eye,
Of tricky, restless infancy?
Ah! many a lightly sportive child,
Who hath like thee our wits beguiled,
To dull and sober manhood grown,
With strange recoil our hearts disown.
Even so, poor kit! must thou endure,
When thou become'st a cat demure,
Full many a cuff and angry word,
Chid roughly from the tempting board,
And yet, for that thou hast, I ween,
So oft our favoured playmate been,
Soft be the change, which thou shalt prove,
When time hath spoiled thee of our love;

Still be thou deem'd, by housewife fat,
A comely, careful, mousing cat,
Whose dish is, for the public good,
Replenish'd oft with savoury food.
Nor, when thy span of life be past,
Be thou to pond or dunghill cast;
But gently borne on goodman's spade,
Beneath the decent sod be laid,
And children show, with glistening eyes,
The place where poor old Pussy lies.

JOANNA BAILLIE (*1762–1851*)

THE KITTEN AND FALLING LEAVES

THAT way look, my Infant, lo!
What a pretty baby-show!
See the Kitten on the wall,
Sporting with the leaves that fall,
Withered leaves—one—two—and three—
From the lofty elder-tree!
Through the calm and frosty air
Of this morning bright and fair,
Eddying round and round they sink
Softly, slowly: one might think,
From the motions that are made,
Every little leaf conveyed
Sylph or Faery hither tending—
To this lower world descending,
Each invisible and mute,
In his wavering parachute.
——But the Kitten, how she starts,
Crouches, stretches, paws, and darts!
First at one, and then its fellow,
Just as light and just as yellow;

There are many now—now one—
Now they stop and there are none:
What intenseness of desire
In her upward eye of fire!
With a tiger-leap half-way
Now she meets the coming prey,
Lets it go as fast, and then
Has it in her power again:
Now she works with three or four,
Like an Indian conjurer;
Quick as he in feats of art,
Far beyond in joy of heart.
Were her antics played in the eye
Of a thousand standers-by,
Clapping hands with shout and stare,
What would little Tabby care
For the plaudits of the crowd?
Over happy to be proud,
Over wealthy in the treasure
Of her own exceeding pleasure!

'Tis a pretty baby-treat;
Nor, I deem, for me unmeet;
Here, for neither Babe nor me,
Other playmate can I see,
Of the countless living things,
That with stir of feet and wings
(In the sun or under shade,
Upon bough or grassy blade)
And with busy revellings,
Chirp and song, and murmurings,
Made this orchard's narrow space,
And this vale, so blithe a place;
Multitudes are swept away
Never more to breathe the day:
Some are sleeping; some in bands
Travelled into distant lands;

Others slunk to moor and wood,
Far from human neighbourhood;
And among the kinds that keep
With us closer fellowship,
With us openly abide,
All have lain their mirth aside.

Where is he that giddy Sprite,
Blue-cap, with his colours bright,
Who was blest as bird could be,
Feeding in the apple-tree;
Made such wanton spoil and rout,
Turning blossoms inside out;
Hung—head pointing towards the ground—
Fluttered, perched, into a round
Bound himself, and then unbound;
Lithest, gaudiest Harlequin!
Prettiest Tumbler ever seen!
Light of heart and light of limb;
What is now become of Him?
Lambs, that through the mountains went
Frisking, bleating merriment,
When the year was in its prime,
They are sobered by this time.
If you look to vale or hill,
If you listen, all is still,
Save a little neighbouring rill,
That from out the rocky ground
Strikes a solitary sound.
Vainly glitter hill and plain,
And the air is calm in vain;
Vainly Morning spreads the lure
Of a sky serene and pure;
Creature none can she decoy
Into open sign of joy:
Is it that they have a fear
Of the dreary season near?

Or that other pleasures be
Sweeter even than gaiety?

Yet, what'er enjoyments dwell
In the impenetrable cell
Of the silent heart which Nature
Furnishes to every creature;
Whatso'er we feel and know
Too sedate for outward show,
Such a light of gladness breaks,
Pretty Kitten! from thy freaks—
Spreads with such a living grace
O'er my little Dora's face;
Yes, the sight so stirs and charms
Thee, Baby, laughing in my arms,
That almost I could repine
That your transports are not mine,
That I do not wholly fare
Even as ye do, thoughtless pair!
And I will have my careless season
Spite of melancholy reason,
Will walk through life in such a way
That, when time brings on decay,
Now and then I may possess
Hours of perfect gladsomeness.
—Pleased by any random toy;
By a kitten's busy joy,
Or an infant's laughing eye
Sharing in the ecstasy;
I would fare like that or this,
Find my wisdom in my bliss;
Keep the sprightly soul awake,
And have faculties to take,
Even from things by sorrow wrought,
Matter for a jocund thought,
Spite of care, and spite of grief,
To gambol with Life's falling leaf.

   WILLIAM WORDSWORTH (*1770–1850*)

VERSES ON A CAT

A CAT in distress,
Nothing more, nor less;
Good folks, I must faithfully tell ye,
As I am a sinner,
It waits for some dinner
To stuff out its own little belly.

You would not easily guess
All the modes of distress
Which torture the tenants of earth;
And the various evils,
Which like so many devils,
Attend the poor souls from their birth.

Some a living require,
And others desire
An old fellow out of the way;
And which is the best
I leave to be guessed,
For I cannot pretend to say.

One wants society,
Another variety,
Others a tranquil life;
Some want food,
Others, as good,
Only want a wife.

But this poor little cat
Only wanted a rat,
To stuff out its own little maw;
And it were as good
Some people had such food,
To make them *hold their jaw*!

PERCY BYSSHE SHELLEY (*1792–1822*)
Juvenilia (1800)

TO A CAT

Cat! who hast pass'd thy grand climacteric,
   How many mice and rats hast in thy days
   Destroy'd?—How many titbits stolen? Gaze
With those bright languid segments green, and prick
Those velvet ears—but prithee do not stick
   Thy latent talons in me—and upraise
   Thy gentle mew—and tell me all thy frays
Of fish and mice, and rats and tender chick.
Nay, look not down, nor lick thy dainty wrists—
   For all the wheezy asthma,—and for all
Thy tail's tip is nick'd off—and though the fists
   Of many a maid have given thee many a maul,
Still is that fur as soft as when the lists
   In youth thou enter'dst on glass bottled wall.

JOHN KEATS (1795–1821)

CATS

The fervent lover and the sage austere
In their ripe season equally admire
The great soft cats, who, like their masters dear,
Are shivery folk and sit beside the fire.

Friends both of learning and of wantonness,
They hunt where silence and dread shadows are;
Erebus would have yoked them to his car
For funeral coursers had their pride been less.

They take, brooding, the noble attitudes
Of sphinxes stretched in deepest solitudes
That look to slumber in an endless dream:
Their loins are quick with kindlings magical,
And glints of gold, as in a sandy stream,
Vaguely bestar their eyeballs mystical.

CHARLES BAUDELAIRE (1821–67)
translated from the French by D. S. MacColl

ATOSSA

An extract from "Poor Matthias"

Poor Matthias! Wouldst thou have
More than pity? claim'st a stave?
—Friends more near us than a bird
We dismiss'd without a word.
Rover, with the good brown head,
Great Atossa, they are dead;
Dead, and neither prose nor rhyme
Tells the praises of their prime.
Thou didst know them old and grey,
Know them in their sad decay.
Thou hast seen Atossa sage
Sit for hours beside thy cage;
Thou wouldst chirp, thou foolish bird,
Flutter, chirp—she never stirr'd!
What were now these toys to her?
Down she sank amid her fur;
Eyed thee with a soul resign'd—
And thou deemedst cats were kind!
—Cruel, but composed and bland,
Dumb, inscrutable and grand,
So Tiberius might have sat,
Had Tiberius been a cat. . . .

MATTHEW ARNOLD (*1822–88*)

LAYS OF TOM-CAT HIDDIGEIGEI

I

When through valley and o'er mountain
Howls the storm at dead of night,
Clambering over roof and chimney,
Hiddigeigei seeks the height;

Spectre-like aloft he stands there,
Fairer than he ever seems;
From his eyes the fire-flame sparkles,
From his bristling hair it streams.

And he lifts his voice, and wildly
Sings an old cat-battle song,
That, like far-off thunder rolling,
Sweeps the storm-vexed night along.

Never a child of man can hear it—
Each sleeps heedless in his house;
But, deep down in darkest cellar,
Hears, and paling, quakes the mouse.

Well she knows the greybeard's war-cry,
Knows the cry she trembles at,
Feels how fearful in his fury
Is the grand old hero-cat.

II

From the tower's topmost angle
On the world I turn my eyes—
Mark, serene, the factions wrangle,
And the parties fall and rise.

And the keen cat's eyes they see there—
And the cat's soul feels the joke—
What dull pranks they cut beneath there,
All those petty pigmy-folk.

But what use? For I can't make 'em
See things from my point of view;
Even should the devil take 'em,
'Twill but be the devil's due.

Human nature! who can bear it?
Crooked ways and wicked wiles!
Wrapt in consciousness of merit,
Sits the tom-cat on the tiles!

> J. V. SCHEFFEL (*1826–86*)
> *translated from the German by William Fitzgerald*

ON THE DEATH OF A CAT,
A FRIEND OF MINE AGED TEN YEARS AND A HALF

WHO shall tell the lady's grief
When her cat was past relief?
Who shall number the hot tears
Shed o'er her, belov'd for years?
Who shall say the dark dismay
Which her dying caused that day?

Come, ye Muses, one and all,
Come obedient to my call;
Come and mourn with tuneful breath
Each one for a separate death;
And, while you in numbers sigh,
I will sing her elegy.

Of a noble race she came,
And Grimalkin was her name.
Young and old full many a mouse
Felt the prowess of her house;
Weak and strong full many a rat
Cowered beneath her crushing pat;
And the birds around the place
Shrank from her too-close embrace.
But one night, reft of her strength,
She lay down and died at length:
Lay a kitten by her side

In whose life the mother died.
Spare her life and lineage,
Guard her kitten's tender age,
And that kitten's name as wide
Shall be known as hers that died.
And whoever passes by
The poor grave where Puss doth lie,
Softly, softly let him tread,
Nor disturb her narrow bed.

    CHRISTINA ROSSETTI (*1830–94*)

TO A CAT

I

STATELY, kindly, lordly friend,
  Condescend
Here to sit by me, and turn
Glorious eyes that smile and burn,
Golden eyes, love's lustrous meed,
On the golden page I read.

All your wondrous wealth of hair,
  Dark and fair,
Silken-shaggy, soft and bright
As the clouds and beams of night,
Pays my reverent hand's caress
Back with friendlier gentleness.

Dogs may fawn on all and some
  As they come;
You, a friend of loftier mind,
Answer friends alone in kind.
Just your foot upon my hand
Softly bids it understand.

Morning round this silent sweet
        Garden-seat
Sheds its wealth of gathering light,
Thrills the gradual clouds with might,
Changes woodland, orchard, heath,
Lawn, and garden there beneath.

Fair and dim they gleamed below:
        Now they glow
Deep as even your sunbright eyes,
Fair as even the wakening skies.
Can it not or can it be
Now that you give thanks to see?

May not you rejoice as I,
        Seeing the sky
Change to heaven revealed, and bid
Earth reveal the heaven it hid
All night long from stars and moon,
Now the sun sets all in tune?

What within you wakes with day
        Who can say?
All too little may we tell,
Friends who like each other well,
What might haply, if we might,
Bid us read our lives aright.

II

Wild on woodland ways your sires
        Flashed like fires;
Fair as flame and fierce and fleet
As with wings on wingless feet
Shone and sprang your mother, free,
Bright and brave as wind or sea.

Free and proud and glad as they,
      Here to-day
Rests or roams their radiant child,
Vanquished not, but reconciled,
Free from curb of aught above
Save the lovely curb of love.

Love through dreams of souls divine
      Fain would shine
Round a dawn whose light and song
Then should right our mutual wrong—
Speak, and seal the love-lit law
Sweet Assisi's seer foresaw.

Dreams were theirs; yet haply may
      Dawn a day
When such friends and fellows born,
Seeing our earth as fair at morn,
May for wiser love's sake see
More of heaven's deep heart than we.
    ALGERNON CHARLES SWINBURNE (*1837–1909*)

LAST WORDS TO A DUMB FRIEND

PET was never mourned as you
Purrer of the spotless hue,
Plumy tail, and wistful gaze
While you humoured our queer ways,
Or outshrilled your morning call
Up the stairs and through the hall—
Foot suspended in its fall—
While expectant, you would stand
Arched to meet the stroking hand;
Till your way you choose to wend
Yonder, to your tragic end.

Never another pet for me!
Let your place all vacant be;
Better blankness day by day
Than companion torn away.
Better bid his memory fade,
Better blot each mark he made,
Selfishly escape distress
By contrived forgetfulness,
Than preserve his prints to make
Every morn and eve an ache.

From the chair whereon he sat
Sweep his fur, nor wince thereat;
Rake his little pathways out
Mid the bushes roundabout;
Smooth away his talons' mark
From the claw-worn pine-tree bark,
Where he climbed as dusk embrowned,
Waiting us who loitered round.

Strange it is this speechless thing,
Subject to our mastering,
Subject for his life and food
To our gift, and time, and mood;
Timid pensioner of us Powers,
His existence ruled by ours,
Should—by crossing at a breath
Into safe and shielded death,
By the merely taking hence
Of his insignificance—
Loom as largened to the sense,
Shape as part, above man's will,
Of the Imperturbable.

As a prisoner, flight debarred,
Exercising in a yard,
Still retain I, troubled, shaken,
Mean estate, by him forsaken;

And this home, which scarcely took
Impress from his little look,
By his faring to the Dim
Grows all eloquent of him.

Housemate, I can think you still
Bounding to the window-sill,
Over which I vaguely see
Your small mound beneath the tree,
Showing in the autumn shade
That you moulder where you played.

THOMAS HARDY (1840–1928)

CAT AND LADY

THEY were at play, she and her cat,
And it was marvellous to mark
The white paw and the white hand pat
Each other in the deepening dark.

The stealthy little lady hid
Under her mittens' silken sheath
Her deadly agate nails that thrid
The silk-like dagger points of death.

The cat purred primly and drew in
Her claws that were of steel filed thin:
The devil was in it all the same.

And in the boudoir, while a shout
Of laughter in the air rang out,
Four sparks of phosphor shone like flame.

PAUL VERLAINE (1844–96)
translated from the French by Arthur Symons

CONNOISSEURS

Under a tree I read a Latin book,
And there, in seeming slumber, lies my cat;
Each of us thinking, with our harmless look,
Of this and that.

Such singing—prettier than any words—
O singers you are sweet and well-to-do!
My cat, who has the finest taste in birds,
Thinks so too.
D. S. MacColl (b. 1859)

TO MY CAT

Half loving-kindliness, and half disdain,
Thou comest to my call serenely suave,
With humming speech and gracious gestures grave,
In salutation courtly and urbane:
Yet must I humble me thy grace to gain—
For wiles may win thee, but no arts enslave,
And nowhere gladly thou abidest save
Where naught disturbs the concord of thy reign.
Sphinx of my quiet hearth! who deignst to dwell,
Friend of my toil, companion of mine ease,
Thine is the lore of Rā and Rameses;
That men forget dost thou remember well,
Beholden still in blinking reveries,
With sombre sea-green eyes inscrutable.
Rosamund Marriott Watson (1863–1911)

ARSINOË'S CATS

*Imitation of the manner of the later Greek poets, c. A.D. 500.
Cats were unknown in historic Greece till about the Christian era.*

ARSINOË the fair, the amber-tressed,
    Is mine no more;
Cold as the unsunned snows are, is her breast,
    And closed her door.
No more her ivory feet and tresses braided
    Make glad mine eyes;
Snapt are my viol strings, my flowers are faded;
    My love-lamp dies.

Yet, once for dewy myrtle-buds and roses,
    All summer long,
We searched the twilight-haunted garden closes
    With jest and song.
Ay, all is over now—my heart hath changéd
    Its heaven for hell;
And that ill chance which all our love estrangéd
    In this wise fell:

A little lion, small and dainty sweet
    (For such there be!),
With sea-grey eyes and softly stepping feet,
    She prayed of me.
For this through lands Egyptian far away
    She bade me pass;
But, in an evil hour, I said her nay—
    And now, alas!
Far-travelled Nicias hath wooed and won
    Arsinoë,
With gifts of furry creatures white and dun
    From over-sea.

              ROSAMUND MARRIOTT WATSON

THE CAT AND THE MOON

The cat went here and there
And the moon spun round like a top,
And the nearest kin of the moon
The creeping cat looked up.
Black Minnaloushe stared at the moon,
For wander and wail as he would
The pure cold light in the sky
Troubled his animal blood.
Minnaloushe runs in the grass,
Lifting his delicate feet.
Do you dance, Minnaloushe, do you dance?
When two close kindred meet
What better than call a dance.
Maybe the moon may learn,
Tired of that courtly fashion,
A new dance turn.
Minnaloushe creeps through the grass
From moonlit place to place,
The sacred moon overhead
Has taken a new phase.
Does Minnaloushe know that his pupils
Will pass from change to change,
And that from round to crescent,
From crescent to round they range?
Minnaloushe creeps through the grass
Alone, important and wise,
And lifts to the changing moon
His changing eyes.

WILLIAM BUTLER YEATS (*1865–1939*)

LE PETIT CHAT

Pert as any young page-boy, the small black cat
Plays on my table, and has the freedom of it;

And there quite motionless sometimes he will sit,
For all the world like a dainty live paper-weight.

Not a hair on his black pelt moving, without a stir,
He rests there long, dead-black on a white leaf,
Like a little toy cat, whose lolling tongue—
A soft felt pad—serves for a pen-wiper.

When he begs—on hind-legs standing—a dainty bear,
I, too, on my hunkers crouching, before him lay
As he stands there with soft clasped paws, his daily fare—
A saucer brimmed with his milky déjeuner.

He sniffs with delicate nose, and—still delicately—
He stirs the surface with tiny lappings of tongue;
Then settling down to the work—deliberately,
Drinks, and one hears the lap, lap, lapping—an undersong.

He drinks, tail waving, and never a pause makes he,
Nor lifts the flat soft muzzle a moment's space,
Till his rough pink tongue has gone most scrupulously
Round and round his saucer, and cleaned it in every place.

Then, licking his whiskers, looks with a wondering air
At a feast that was too soon ended, but sudden he sees
Some splashes—white on the black—and, with extreme care,
Starts anew to rid his tarnished splendour of these.

Then peering, as though short-sighted, through half-closed eyes
(That gleam, blue and yellow, like agates, when opened wide),
Snorts, and suddenly jumping, with muzzle in paws he lies
Stretched at full length, like a tiger, upon his side.

EDMOND ROSTAND (1868–1918)
translated from the French by Seumas O'Sullivan

FIVE EYES

In Hans' old mill his three black cats
Watch the bins for thieving rats.
Whisker and claw, they crouch in the night,
Their five eyes smouldering green and bright:
Squeaks from the flour-sacks, squeaks from where
The cold wind stirs on the empty stair,
Squeaking and scampering everywhere.
Then down they pounce, now in, now out,
At whisking tail, and sniffing snout;
While lean old Hans he snores away
Till peep of light at break of day;
Then up he climbs to his creaking mill.
Out come his cats all grey with meal—
Jekkel, and Jessup, and one-eyed Jill.

WALTER DE LA MARE (*b. 1873*)

TONY'S GRAVE

"*Qui nunc it per iter tenebricosum*" (Catullus, 3)

My golden comrade, since I could not save
Your soft small paws from treading the last road
Which all must take, I lay you in this grave
By the high garden wall, where oft you sat
In the long summer sunlight indolent,
Yet mindful too, my predatory cat,
Of things that fluttered in the bushes near,
Or, worthier foeman, the sleek water rat
That, darting through the tangled couch-grass, went
To his moist cavern by the water-side
Unseen of all but you. But this I pray,
As you go down to Lethe's waveless tide,
If you should meet with one small shivering ghost
That once was Lesbia's sparrow, sheathe your claws—

Sheathe them in velvet well, remembering
That you too were a lover. Many a night
You left the hearth-rug warmth, the garish light,
My books and me—after due toilet made
With small rough tongue, and wetted paw (for these,
My Tony, were the things that served you most
In place of all the things that mortals use),
To spring into the darkness unafraid,
Seeking adventure where an earlier time
Saw loves less innocent and beaux less kind.
So fare thee well. The dark that none can stay
Awaits the sunset of our mortal day—
Ah, not Catullus, not *that* Lesbia knew
A thing more exquisitely fine than you.

     SEUMAS O'SULLIVAN (*b. 1878*)

A CAT

SHE had a name among the children;
But no one loved though some one owned
Her, locked her out of doors at bedtime,
And had her kittens duly drowned.

In spring, nevertheless, this cat
Ate blackbirds, thrushes, nightingales,
And birds of bright voice, and plume, and flight,
As well as scraps from neighbours' pails.

I loathed and hated her for this;
One speckle on a thrush's breast
Was worth a million such; and yet
She lived long till God gave her rest.

     EDWARD THOMAS (*1878–1917*)

MILK FOR THE CAT

When the tea is brought at five o'clock,
And all the neat curtains are drawn with care,
The little black cat with bright green eyes
Is suddenly purring there.

At first she pretends, having nothing to do,
She has come in merely to blink by the grate,
But though tea may be late or the milk may be sour,
She is never late.

And presently her agate eyes
Take a soft large milky haze,
And her independent casual glance
Becomes a stiff, hard gaze.

Then she stamps her claws or lifts her ears
Or twists her tail and begins to stir,
Till suddenly all her lithe body becomes
One breathing, trembling purr.

The children eat and wriggle and laugh;
The two old ladies stroke their silk:
But the cat is grown small and thin with desire,
Transformed to a creeping lust for milk.

The white saucer like some full moon descends
At last from the cloud of the table above;
She sighs and dreams and thrills and glows,
Transfigured with love.

She nestles over the shining rim,
Buries her chin in the creamy sea;
Her tail hangs loose; each drowsy paw
Is doubled under each bending knee.

A long dim ecstasy holds her life;
Her world is an infinite shapeless white,
Till her tongue has curled the last holy drop
Then she sinks back into the night,

Draws and dips her body to heap
Her sleepy nerves in the great arm-chair,
Lies defeated and buried deep
Three or four hours unconscious there.

    HAROLD MONRO (*1879–1932*)

CAT'S MEAT

Ho, all you cats in all the street;
Look out, it is the hour of meat:

The little barrow is crawling along,
And the meat-boy growling his fleshy song.

Hurry, Ginger! Hurry, White!
Don't delay to court or fight.

Wandering Tabby, vagrant Black,
Yamble from adventure back!

Slip across the shining street,
Meat! Meat! Meat! Meat!

Lift your tail and dip your feet;
Find your penny—Meat! Meat!

Where's your mistress? Learn to purr
Pennies emanate from her.

Be to her, for she is Fate,
Perfectly affectionate.

(You, domestic Pinkie-Nose,
Keep inside, and warm your toes.)

Flurry, flurry in the street—
Meat! Meat! Meat! Meat!

HAROLD MONRO

THE CAT

DEAR creature by the fire a-purr,
   Strange idol eminently bland,
Miraculous puss! As o'er your fur
   I trail a negligible hand,

And gaze into your gazing eyes,
   And wonder in a demi-dream
What mystery it is that lies
   Behind those slits that glare and gleam,

An exquisite enchantment falls
   About the portals of my sense;
Meandering through enormous halls
   I breathe luxurious frankincense,

An ampler air, a warmer June
   Enfold me, and my wondering eye
Salutes a more imperial moon
   Throned in a more resplendent sky

Than ever knew this northern shore.
   O, strange! For you are with me too,
And I who am a cat once more
   Follow the woman that was you.

With tail erect and pompous march,
   The proudest puss that ever trod,
Through many a grove, 'neath many an arch,
   Impenetrable as a god,

Down many an alabaster flight
Of broad and cedar-shaded stairs,
While over us the elaborate night
Mysteriously gleams and glares!

Lytton Strachey (1880–1932)

PHIL, THE BLACK PERSIAN

Philander's a king, a dandy king
In his ruffle and furry gown;
And his eyes are bright as the clear moonlight
When the dusk steals over the town.
O, a king is he, as you soon will see,
And I am his Nubian slave;
He never would give up a thing for me,
And I fear that he'd purr on my grave.

Philander's a king, a glamorous king,
When he climbs to the moon o' nights.
In the day may be seen that his eyeballs are green
But at dusk they are lunar lights.
" O, Moon! " warbles he, " O, Cynthia! we
Are the splendidest things on high,
For I am king of this gabled sea,
While you are the queen of the sky."

Philander's a king, a dusky king,
In his mantle as sable as night's;
Yet his paws are like snow, though always he'll go
And smudge them in cinder fights;
But kings must wage war with tooth and claw,
As you'll hear in the midnight's beat
When the warrior toms with rolling drums
Come marching along the street.

Philander's a king, a tyrannous king,
And I am his Nubian slave:
I must bring him milk and a pillow of silk,
All things that a king may crave,
I must warm the milk, I must straighten the silk,
I must bend and balance and kneel
To the king with the claws in the amorous paws
And the eyes like staring steel.

HERBERT PALMER (*b. 1880*)

ON A CAT AGING

He blinks upon the hearth-rug
And yawns in deep content,
Accepting all the comforts
That Providence has sent.

Louder he purrs, and louder,
In one glad hymn of praise,
For all the night's adventures,
For quiet, restful days.

Life will go on for ever,
With all that cat can wish;
Warmth, and the glad procession
Of fish, and milk and fish.

Only—the thought disturbs him—
He's noticed once or twice,
The times are somehow breeding
A nimbler race of mice.

ALEXANDER GRAY (*b. 1882*)

CAT AND CROCUSES

In the crocus-bed I saw her;
Like a queen enthroned she sat.
Yellow crocuses shone round her—
Royal, sun-illumined cat:

Orange eyes intensely lighted
By a vivid golden flame:
Fire of spring that burnt within her,
And in every flower the same.

World-surveying, world-contented,
Seated in her crocus-ring:
Cat and crocuses together
Basking in the fires of spring.

　　　　　　　EVA MARTIN (*b. 1883*)

ON MAOU DYING AT THE AGE OF SIX MONTHS

STRANGE sickness fell upon this perfect creature
Who walked the equal friend of Man and Nature.
Her little Bodie, e'en as by a shroud,
Lay lapped in its unseen, dishevelling cloud;
Till to her eyes, unasking but afraid,
The old reply of endless night was made.

　　　　　　FRANCES CORNFORD (*b. 1886*)

STREET OF CATS

(New York City)
1912

CLOSE the high-stooped houses stood
In that quiet neighbourhood,
Undisturbed by trucks or vans,
Pushcarts with their fruit and pans,

Scavengers with sticks and bags,
Or the junk-man crying " Rags "—
No, not even gutter-brats;
But at night it swarmed with cats;
Slinking cats and blinking cats,
Cats to chase and cats to clamber
(Eyes like topaz, eyes like amber)
Round about each garbage can,
In and out of areas ran;
Scrawny cats, with deep aversion
To the Maltese and the Persian
(Soft and sleek that purr and mew
Where the wealthy avenue
Boasts its brownstone " No admittance! "
To all ragged stranger kittens).

Here, as street lamps sparked and spluttered
Down the cobbled street unguttered,
Shade to glare and glare to shade
Moved the feline promenade,
Brindled, blacker than the Devil,
Toms and tabbies in a revel,
Like familiars known to witches,
Like the mouser brought such riches
To Dick Whittington in history,
Like Egyptian cats of mystery,
Crouching, scampering, stalking, squawling,
Spitting fire or caterwauling,
Licking sores, rampant or sleeping—
'Faith it set my skin to creeping
As I viewed them perched on high,
In my window next the sky!

Every window blankly glistened
And the dark street slept and listened.
Clap-clap-clap: a footfall faint;
Then the Elevated's plaint

Grinding on a curve afar;
Then a distant surface car
Jarring past; a cop's night-stick
Rapping quickly on the brick,
Meanwhile—cats—in swirling mazes
Through the harbour-fog's night hazes
That came seeping from the river,
Setting dainty dreams a-shiver
To the long, lugubrious moaning
Of the river craft intoning—
Cats that overflowed each curbing
With an aimlessness disturbing,
Prowling, yowling; yowling, prowling;
With such grinning and such scowling!
Cat Luculluses that sought
In much refuse, feasts unbought;
Cats that wooed and cats that fought.

O for some black plague of rats
That would rid my street of cats!

They would slither 'twixt your feet,
Coming home along the street.
As you fumbled for your keys
They would stalk by twos and threes
Like fierce bandits at your back,
Wildly whiskered, cloaked in black.
They would haunt the steps thereafter
Spreading scandal, faint with laughter
Of a still demoniac kind
That was never to my mind.
And their cries, so strangely human—
Gasping child—heartbroken woman!

So one's dreams (each dawn upbraided)
With gigantic cats paraded;
Cats that walked the moonlit sill
In a pageant never still,

Cats that writhing seemed to rise
From the street and fill the skies
Like a locust-cloud by day,
Like a feline Milky Way,
Where the moon, great puss of space,
With one cloud-paw washed its face,
Licked its lips and grinned again
Down on scampering mice and men!

    WILLIAM ROSE BENÉT (*b. 1886*)

BAST

SHE had green eyes, that excellent seer,
And little peaks to either ear.
She sat there, and I sat here.

She spoke of Egypt, and a white
Temple, against enormous night.

She smiled with clicking teeth and said
That the dead were never dead;

Said old emperors hung like bats
In barns at night, or ran like rats—
But empresses came back as cats!

    WILLIAM ROSE BENÉT

MACAVITY: THE MYSTERY CAT

MACAVITY's a Mystery Cat: he's called the Hidden Paw—
For he's the master criminal who can defy the Law.
He's the bafflement of Scotland Yard, the Flying Squad's despair,
For when they reach the scene of crime—" Macavity's not
 there!"

Macavity, Macavity, there's no one like Macavity,
He's broken every human law, he breaks the law of gravity.
His powers of levitation would make a fakir stare,
And when you reach the scene of crime—" Macavity's not there! "
You may seek him in the basement, you may look up in the air—
But I tell you once and once again, " Macavity's not there! "

Macavity's a ginger cat, he's very tall and thin;
You would know him if you saw him, for his eyes are sunken in.
His brow is deeply lined with thought, his head is highly domed,
His coat is dusty from neglect, his whiskers are uncombed.
He sways his head from side to side, with movements like a snake,
And when you think he's half asleep he's always wide awake.

Macavity, Macavity, there's no one like Macavity,
For he's a fiend in feline shape, a monster of depravity,
You may meet him in a by-street, you may see him in the square—
But when a crime's discovered, then " Macavity's not there! "

He's outwardly respectable. (They say he cheats at cards.)
And his footprints are not found in any file of Scotland Yard's,
And when the larder's looted, or the jewel-case is rifled,
Or when the milk is missing, or another Peke's been stifled,
Or the greenhouse glass is broken, and the trellis past repair—
Ay, there's the wonder of the thing! " Macavity's not there! "

And when the Foreign Office find a Treaty's gone astray,
Or the Admiralty lose some plans and drawings by the way,
There may be a scrap of paper in the hall or on the stair—
But it's useless to investigate—" Macavity's not there! "
And when the loss has been disclosed the Secret Service say:
" It *must* have been Macavity! "—but he's half a mile away.
You'll be sure to find him resting, or a-licking of his thumbs,
Or engaged in doing complicated long-division sums.

Macavity, Macavity, there's no one like Macavity,
There never was a Cat of such deceitfulness and suavity.
He always has an alibi, and one or two to spare:
At whatever time the deed took place—*Macavity wasn't there*!
And they say that all the Cats whose wicked deeds are widely
    known
(I might mention Mungojerrie, I might mention Griddlebone)
Are nothing more than agents for the Cat who all the time
Just controls their operations: the Napoleon of Crime!

T. S. ELIOT (*b. 1888*)

BUNCH: A CAT

I opened a book
And on the white glossed page
    Are the two brown pads
        You made.

Down the garden path
I watch the delicate tread
Of your feathered feet round the little bright pools
    And your questioning head;
    I see your body sweep
Up the trunk and along the green boughs
    Of the apple-trees,
  Then a clawed pad dip to thrust
At the hand that gently shakes a branch beneath,
    And your beating, swaying brush.

And still with shivering desire you creep
Where angry sparrows shrill battles in the peas,
    Where the fledgling thrushes hide,
Or the bold chaffinch tempts with frantic cheep and chide
  From his nesting mate in the elder-tree.

A hundred times in vain you poise, you leap;
    Crestfallen, stand denied.
  Yet too often a broken body hangs
  Limp in your tiger fangs.

Or you stalk, ever nearer and nearer,
White butterflies that flit in the sun
From sweet alyssum to fragrant phlox,
From crimson snapdragons to lofty hollyhocks;
  And the warm dusk June nights every one
You lie deep hid in the mowing grass
Till the little white moths float crazily by
  And you follow running, leaping high.

    After milk is lapped
  By the winter fireside, on the rug,
And the dangled hare's foot tempts to no game,
  On my knees you settle snug,
  Warm bunch of sweet-smelling fur,
And with rushing wind, clock tick, rustle of flame
  Drowses your sing-song purr.

    You'll not come again
    In your dear imperious way
  To drum at the window-pane
      On a rainy day;
    Never bite, clutch, kick
The hand a small rough tongue would after lick;
    No wind shall stir
The soft luxuriance, your tawny fur;
In your Spring, in your body's pride,
  We found you in your form,
    Curled in your wonted bed
      Asleep and warm,
        But dead.

              CLAUDE COLLEER ABBOTT (*b. 1889*)

PASSAGE ON

Farewell, most charming of females,
Good hunting wherever you may be,
And may you find your hundred murdered babies!
How you excelled in our most vaunted virtues:
Of kindliness and gentleness, of self-effacing,
Giving: and what wisdom singly shone from your one eye!
Charming were your manners and dainty your moving.
Though you were not a well-bred cat,
Who better understood the laws of home or hearth
And who the niceness of a welcome greeting,
However strange the guest?

You ruled this house, ruling with your soft insistence
Both cat and man; were faithful to your shabby Tom,
Polite to hens and never spoiled my flowers;
Asking nothing but a little food, and such attention
As all women do.

I think that even Death himself,
Looking into that wise eye,
Could not have dared to hurt you very much.
Surely when I too am dead and wandering,
I should happen on Cat Paradise
And, knocking, ask the keeper of the gate
For Mrs Peace:
Then you would come and gently welcome me.

Cedric Morris (*b. 1889*)

CAT OF CATS

Now Tom's translated, not a mouse
Dare inhabit Heaven's house;
Cherubim shall bring him milk,
Seraphs stroke his coat of silk

While, with whiskers aureoled,
He shall walk the streets of gold
Or, happily relaxed, lie prone,
Deeply purring, by the throne.

Vivien Bulkley (*b. 1890*)

TO A PERSIAN CAT

So dear, so dainty, so demure,
So charming in whate'er position;
By race the purest of the pure,
A little cat of high condition:
Her coat lies not in trim-kept rows
Of carpet-like and vulgar sleekness:
But like a ruffled sea it grows
Of wavy grey (my special weakness):
She vexes not the night with squalls
That make one seize a boot and throw it:
She joins in no unseemly brawls
(At least she never lets me know it!);
She never bursts in at the door
In manner boisterous and loud:
But silently along the floor
She passes, like a little cloud.
Then, opening wide her amber eyes,
Puts an inquiring nose up—
Sudden upon my knee she flies,
Then purrs and tucks her little toes up.
Yet did she once, as I recall,
By Love's o'ermastering power impelled,
Scale Mr C.'s back-garden wall—
A feat before unparalleled—
Alas! the faithless Tom had flown:
Yet on she glides, with body pliant:
And then, when bidden to come down,
Stood half alarmed and half defiant;

One sudden spring sufficed to land her—
When to return she condescended—
Upon my landlord's glass verandah—
I don't suppose they've had it mended!
This set of verses, Puss, to you
I dedicate—and ask in quittance
One thing alone—'tis nothing new—
A set of quarter-Persian kittens.

   F. C. W. HILEY (*nineteenth century*)

MIKE

ALL ye that learnèd hours beguile
In the Museum's dingy pile,
And daily through its portals pass,
And mark the cat upon the grass
That sat—alas, he sits no more!
Give ear a moment, I implore,
And mourn the fate of poor old Mike!
When shall we ever see his like?
No fate untimely snatched away
This pussy-cat Methusaleh:
For—since we are a learnèd crew
In the Museum—Michael knew
Of Argus, that famed hound of old
Who lived through hunger, heat, and cold;
And when his lord came home at last,
When twenty years were well-nigh past,
Looked up, and wagged his tail, and died:
But Michael, stiff with feline pride,
Vowed, by a dog he'd not be beat
And set himself to cap that feat.
He'd sit and sun himself sedately,
No Sphinx nor Sekhmet looked more stately;
He cared not in the very least
For human being, bird, or beast;

He let the pigeons eat their fill,
Nor even one was known to kill;
But scared them if they strayed too nigh
By the sole terror of his eye.
To public, and officials too,
He showed the scorn which was their due:
And if perchance some forward minx
Dared to go up and stroke the Sphinx—
Her hand shot back, all marked with scores
From the offended Michael's claws.
And he who writes these lines one day
Ventured a compliment to pay,
And for reply received a bite—
No doubt you'll answer, " Serve him right ":
So out of all the human crew
He cared for none—save only two:
For these he purred, for these he played,
And let himself be stroked, and laid
Aside his anti-human grudge:
His owner—and Sir Ernest Budge!
A master of Egyptian lore,
No doubt Sir Ernest had a store
Of charms and spells decipherèd
From feline mummies long since dead,
And found a way by magic art
To win that savage feline heart,
Each morn Sir Ernest, without qualms,
Would take up Michael in his arms;
And still remained his staunchest friend,
And comforted his latter end.
Old Mike, farewell! We all regret you,
Although you would not let us pet you:
Of cats the wisest, oldest, best cat,
This be your motto—*Requiescat!*

F. C. W. HILEY

KITTENS

Airy as leaves blown by the autumn storm,
They sprawl and frolic over the smooth grass,
Each one minutely fashioned in the form
Of feline princes of the wilderness.
The panther and the leopard and the lynx
Are imaged unmistakably in these—
The lion in the shadow of the Sphinx,
The tiger blazing forth from tropic trees.

The tendril limbs, the suave paws, soft as rain,
Recall, with every stir, similitudes
Prowling the pathless bush, the untrodden plain,
Lurking and roving in primeval woods.
The quivering stealth, the sudden pouncing springs,
The wrestling joy, the lithe grace, all betray
The ancestry of fierce untrammelled kings,
Hunting through boundless wastes, predestined prey.

The petal-ears, the eyes' quick moonstone spark,
The shell-frail jaws, the downy new-licked fur,
Each tiniest feature bears the subtle mark
Of some unvanquished forest forefather;
And, as the slight shell-echo faintly rhymes
The mighty clamour of the crashing waves,
Each purring throat diminutively mimes
The growling thunder heard in desert caves.

These are the manifest proud-blooded scions
Of beasts depicted in Assyrian rock,
The true descendants of the Hittite lions
Stone-couched in porticoes of Antioch.
And moulded in no other shape than this,
In coloured brick, great cats perambulate
Along the murals of Persepolis,
Upon the towers of the Ishtar Gate.

These silken puppets, light as puffs of smoke,
Are heirs-apparent of the fabled race
That pranced and reared in Dionysos' yoke
Across the fields of India and Thrace.
These are the wild's exiled inheritors,
Of Asian grace, of splendour African,
The breed of tameless jungle emperors,
That ruled before the dynasties of man.

MICHAEL SCOT (*b. 1891*)

CHARCOAL SKETCH

UPLIFTING suddenly slim fiery-golden anthers,
Scarlet hibiscus-buds of Indian dawn unfolded,
And in their deep-blue-shadowed jungle lair, dark panthers
Unlidded waking eyes, more fiercely fiery-golden.

The hidden stormwind of their tautened muscles moved
Under the thundercloud of drowsy velvet fur,
Carving sleek lissom flanks with hungry ribs and grooves,
Chiselling silken limbs to frolic hunting curves.

Sleepily flaring open yawning sable jaws,
They gaped abysmal caves, flaming geranium,
And tossing slumber-dusk from sun-glossed lazy paws,
Outsprayed the sabre claws, ablaze with mirrored sun.

. . . . . .

Their sun-awakened splendour dazzled in the room
Just for a timeless instant when the firelight broke,
Suddenly smouldering, from midnight charcoal gloom,
Blossoming glowingly through grey enclouding smoke,

Unfolding delicately, scarlet ember buds,
Lifting thin anther-flames of mimic Eastern dawn,
Waking the young black cat upon the sapphire rug
To open fiery-golden eyes, and, stretching, yawn.

MICHAEL SCOT

THE GREATER CATS

The greater cats with golden eyes
Stare out between the bars.
Deserts are there, and different skies,
And night with different stars.
They prowl the aromatic hill,
And mate as fiercely as they kill,
And hold the freedom of their will
To roam, to live, to drink their fill;
But this beyond their wit know I:
Man loves a little, and for long shall die.

Their kind across the desert range
Where tulips spring from stones,
Not knowing they will suffer change
Or vultures pick their bones.
Their strength's eternal in their sight,
They rule the terror of the night,
They overtake the deer in flight,
And in their arrogance they smite;
But I am sage, if they are strong:
Man's love is transient as his death is long.

Yet oh, what powers to deceive!
My wit is turned to faith,
And at this moment I believe
In love, and scout at death.
I came from nowhere, and shall be
Strong, steadfast, swift, eternally:
I am a lion, a stone, a tree,
And as the Polar star in me
Is fixed my constant heart on thee.
Ah, may I stay for ever blind
With lions, tigers, leopards, and their kind.

V. Sackville-West (*b. 1892*)

WAR CAT

I AM sorry, my little cat, I am sorry—
If I had it, you should have it;
But there is a war on.

No, there are no table-scraps;
there was only an omelette
made from dehydrated eggs,
and baked apples to follow,
and we finished it all.
The butcher has no lights,
the fishmonger has no cod's heads—
there is nothing for you
but cat-biscuit
and those remnants of yesterday's ham;
you must do your best with it.

Round and pathetic eyes,
baby mouth opened in a reproachful cry,
how can I explain to you?
I know, I know:
" Mistress, it is not nice;
the ham is very salt
and the cat-biscuit very dull,
I sniffed at it, and the smell was not enticing.
Do you not love me any more?
Mistress, I do my best for the war-effort;
I killed four mice last week,
yesterday I caught a young stoat,
you stroked and praised me,
you called me a clever cat,
What have I done to offend you?
I am industrious, I earn my keep;
I am not like the parrot, who sits there
using bad language and devouring
parrot-seed at eight-and-sixpence a pound
without working for it.

If you will not pay me my wages
there is no justice;
If you have ceased to love me
there is no charity.

" See, now, I rub myself against your legs
to express my devotion,
which is not altered by any unkindness.
My little heart is contracted
because your goodwill is withdrawn from me;
my ribs are rubbing together
for lack of food,
but indeed I cannot eat this—
my soul revolts at the sight of it.
I have tried, believe me,
but it was like ashes in my mouth.
If your favour is departed
and your bowels of compassion are shut up,
then all that is left me
is to sit in a draught on the stone floor and look
    miserable
till I die of starvation
and a broken heart."

Cat with the innocent face,
What can I say?
Everything is very hard on everybody.
If you were a little Greek cat,
or a little Polish cat,
there would be nothing for you at all,
not even cat-food:
indeed, you would be lucky
if you were not eaten yourself.
Think if you were a little Russian cat
prowling among the cinders of a deserted city!
Consider that pains and labour
and the valour of merchant-seamen and fishermen

have gone even to the making of this biscuit
which smells so unappetising.
Alas! there is no language
in which I can tell you these things.

Well, well!
if you will not be comforted
we will put the contents of your saucer
into the chicken-bowl—there!
all gone! nasty old cat-food—
The hens, I dare say,
will be grateful for it.

Wait only a little
and I will go to the butcher
and see if by any chance
he can produce some fragments of the insides of
    something.

Only stop crying
and staring in that unbearable manner—
as soon as I have put on my hat
we will try to do something about it.

My hat is on,
I have put on my shoes,
I have taken my shopping basket—
What are you doing on the table?

The chicken-bowl is licked clean;
there is nothing left in it at all.
Cat,
hell-cat, Hitler-cat, human,
all-too-human cat,
cat corrupt, infected,
instinct with original sin,
cat of a fallen and perverse creation,
hypocrite with the innocent and limpid eyes—

is nothing desirable
till somebody else desires it?

Is anything and everything attractive
so long as it is got by stealing?
Furtive and squalid cat,
green glance, squinted over a cringing shoulder,
streaking hurriedly out of the back door
in expectation of judgment,
your manners and morals are perfectly abhorrent to me,
you dirty little thief and liar.

Nevertheless,
although you have made a fool of me,
yet, bearing in mind your pretty wheedling ways
(not to mention the four mice and the immature stoat),
and having put on my hat to go to the butcher's,
I may as well go.
                DOROTHY L. SAYERS (*b. 1893*)

TO A SIAMESE CAT
(*June* 1930–*December* 1942)

I SHALL walk in the sun alone
Whose golden light you loved:
I shall sleep alone
And stirring touch an empty place:
I shall write uninterrupted—
I would that your gentle paw
Could stay my moving pen just once again!

I shall see beauty,
But none to match your living grace:
I shall hear music,
But not so sweet as the droning song
With which you loved me.

I shall fill my days,
But I shall not, cannot forget:
Sleep soft, dear friend,
For while I live, you shall not die.

    MICHAEL JOSEPH (*b. 1897*)

THE KITTEN'S ECLOGUE

AUCTOR

TELL now, good kit, of three months' age, or less,
Whence dost thou bring thy perfect blessedness?
Beast which must perish, and all black to view,
What makes the happiness of such as you?

BOGY BABY

My sable hue, like Ethiopian queen,
My raven tincture and my jetty dye,
Not as defect or blemish can be seen
By anybody that hath half an eye.
What sight more welcome than the night above?
What hue more honoured in the courts of love?

Unseen at night I ramble, being black,
And against black you will not hear me rail.
They kept the sooty whelp for fortune's sake
When all my stripy brethren plumbed the pail.
Their mice I kill, I stuff me with their tuck,
And no man kicks me lest he spoil his luck.

The sex, which some a sorry burthen deem,
I glory in, and mightily rejoice;
Though but a babe, before the fire I dream
Already that I hear my lover's voice;
What music shall I have—what dying wails—
The seldom female in a world of males!

And when love's star above the chimneys shines,
And in my heart I feel the sacred fire,
Upon the ridge-tile will I hymn these lines
With which great Venus doth my soul inspire;
Then see the toms, in gallant cavalcade,
Come flying to the lovesick fair one's aid!

What mortal dame, what merely human she,
What strong enchantress, could thus honoured sit;
What maid could draw her suitors on like me,
Sing such a tune and get away with it?
What charmer could men's souls so nearly touch?
What nymph, I ask, could do one half as much?

Hold me not foul for that I wanton be.
These amorous frolics are but innocence;
I court no tickle immortality,
And fear no judgment when I go from hence:
No hope, no dread my little grave contains,
Nor anything beside my scant remains!

BOGY BABY'S EMBLEM. O felis semper felix!
EVERYBODY ELSE'S EMBLEM. MUD.

RUTH PITTER (b. 1897)

THE MATRON CAT'S SONG

So once again the trouble's o'er
   And here I sit and sing;
Forgetful of my paramour
   And the pickle I was in;
Lord, lord, it is a trying time
   We bear when we're expecting,
When folk reproach us for the crime
   And frown with glance correcting.

So purra wurra, purra wurra, pronkum pronkum:
   Purra wurra pronkum, pronkum purr.

How much I feared my kits would be
   Slain in the hour of birth!
And so I sought a sanctuary
   Which causes me some mirth;
The surly cook, who hates all cats,
   Hath here a little closet,
And here we nest among her hats—
   Lord save me when she knows it!

Hey purra wurra, etc.

Four kits have I of aspect fair,
   Though usually but three;
Two female tabs, a charming pair,
   Who much resemble me;
Lord, lord, to think upon the sport
   Which doth await the hussies,
They'll be no better than they ought
   Nor worse than other pussies.

O purra wurra, etc.

Yet as becomes a mother fond
   I dote upon my boys,
And think they will excel beyond
   All other toms in noise;
How harsh their manly pelts will be,
   How stern and fixed each feature—
If they escape that cruelty
   Which man doth work on nature!

Ah purra wurra, etc.

Those eyes which now are sealèd fast
   Nine days against the light
Shall ere few months are overpast
   Like stars illume the night;

Those voices that with feeble squall
    Demand my whole attention,
Shall earn with rousing caterwaul
    Dishonourable mention.

Then purra wurra, etc.

But then, alas, I shall not care
    How flighty they may be,
For ere they're grown I'll have to bear
    Another four, or three;
And after all, they are the best
    While the whole crew reposes
With fast-shut eyes, weak limbs at rest,
    And little wrinkled noses.

So purra wurra, purra wurra, pronkum pronkum:
    Purra wurra pronkum, pronkum ryestraw:
Pronkum ryestraw, pronkum ryestraw,
    Pur-ra—wur-ra—pronkum
Pronk . . . Foof.

        (She sleeps.)

                Ruth Pitter

QUORUM PORUM [1]

In a dark Garden, by a dreadful Tree,
The Druid Toms were met. They numbered three:
Tab Tiger, Demon Black, and Ginger Hate.
Their forms were tense, their eyes were full of fate.
Save for the involuntary caudal thrill,
The horror was that they should sit so still.
An hour of ritual silence passed: then low
And marrow-freezing, Ginger moaned Orow,

    [1] 'Porum,' genitive plural of 'Puss.'

Two horrid syllables of hellish lore,
Followed by deeper silence than before.
Another hour, the tabby's turn is come:
Rigid, he rapidly howls MUM MUM MUM,
Then reassumes his silence like a pall,
Clothed in negation, a dumb oracle.
At the third hour, the Black gasps out AH BLURK
Like a lost soul that founders in the mirk,
And the grim, ghastly, damned, and direful crew
Resumes its voiceless vigilance anew.
The fourth hour passes. Suddenly all three
Chant WEGGY WEGGY WEGGY mournfully,
Then stiffly rise, and melt into the shade,
Their Sabbath over, and their demons laid.

RUTH PITTER

THE SAFETY-VALVE

Now baby-talk for babies is taboo,
And Baby must be Fotheringham to you,
Not muzzer's ickle precious any more—
The cats come in for it. It's not a bore
To them; in fact, the stuff is highly prized.
They hog it, but are not demoralized.
Even in households where a word of slang
Provokes the tyrant's frown, the scholar's fang,
No one demurs when bucketsful of gab
Are emptied in a sugared flood on Tab.

And personally I think it's no bad thing
For people who can't act, or swear, or sing,
To have old F. Domesticus for theme—
A grand excuse to let off psychic steam.

He is so pronkum, and his pitty nose
Is finished in such darling shades of rose;

His pads so tippity, his peepy face
(Look, like a baby's, with this bit of lace)
So yumsome, and that mimsy mouth of his
So cupid, that we must go kiss, kiss, kiss.
(Our germs can't hurt him, nor his germs hurt us—
If it were Fotheringham, there'd be a fuss).
His bellikins, all set with little studs
(Mind where you comb) like tiny coral buds.
His pretty sit-upon and cherub thighs,
And most of all his love-love-lovely eyes,
Make all of us so feeble and so fain
That not an inhibition can remain.

Tab purrs in bliss, for he can use it all:
Hark! what was that? I think I hear a squall;
But it evokes only a careless Damn,
The distant howl of lonely Fotheringham.

RUTH PITTER

THE CAT AND THE MAN

BRAITH fach—a half-stone in the scales—
The peerless cat I found in Wales,
Lithe, daring, cleanly, nimble, neat
Unostentatious, arch, discreet,
A model Dürer would have limned,
Her eyes dark suns with amber rimmed,
In mottled coat of jet and ermine,
She rid our Wicklow glen of vermin,
Bred the best mousers in the land—
Supply could never meet demand.
Though kestrel-quick with teeth and talons
To help in keeping Nature's balance,
She mastered too the art of giving
And well-conducted graceful living.

When Malachy Moore is out of a job
Or fresh from the lock-up, the greasy swab
Spends his sober moments snaring rabbits.
That is the kindliest of his habits.
For Moore's compact of spite and hate,
With bleary scowl and lurching gait,
With leprous skin, and a leathery lug
Projecting each side of his taciturn mug.
With lips that dribble and eyes that skelly,
A bridgeless nose and a pendulous belly;
His drunkenness is the talk of the town,
And the smell of his breath would knock you down;
A sly vindictive sod, no laggard
At firing ricks, a thief and blackguard
Disliked from mountain-top to coast,
And Thor our dog dislikes him most.
Let writhing conies twitch their scuts
That Moore may stuff his stinking guts;
Or rot with gangrene in the field
To make the pence their tortures yield.

The speckled cat, on forage maybe—
Mindful of her remaining baby—
One twilight when the woods were bare
Put her left forefoot in Moore's snare.
A broken paw and blinding pain
For twenty hours in sleet and rain:
" A good catch," so the devils name it,
And laugh if sentimentals blame it.
A night and day passed slowly by.
We might have sought her, Thor and I.
I stand unshriven till I die.

Braith, struggling, loosens the snare's peg,
Limps home bedraggled with gashed leg.
The vets came in from round about

To try to drive the poison out
That soon appears, in languid gaze
And fevered blood and listless ways.
But drug and salve and surgeon's lance
Will not bring back that golden glance.
The wide and wondering eyes are dim,
As feeling fails in every limb
Precisely flecked and smoothly furred
(Deep in its corner her kitten purred).
For all that vets could do or say,
Cath Braith died on the seventh day,
My fearless fighter and famous ratter,
So that Malachy Moore may grow fatter and fatter,
He's killed my poem-in-black-and-white,
Dealt savage death to wild delight.

I pray for patience, wisdom's lore.
Men rule I shall not murder Moore,
Not use the gun or sudden knife
To terminate his worthless life.
The part is greater than the whole:
I must not launch his sacred soul
Across the bounds of space and time,
In hope it reach some warmer clime.
You gods who set each creature's task,
In humble deference I ask
Which clearer saw your primal plan,
The cat or this immortal man.

OLIVER EDWARDS (b. 1900)

BLACK CAT IN PRUNUS-TREE

DARK demon angel, by royal right
Sits Satan in a world of light
Where buds have broken, starry white.

Bowered in prunus, blackest Puss,
Set in snow branches, crouching thus,
Brings Night's small island home to us.

Two orange planets his eyes glow
Down at the spaniel's leaps below.
No stir will cat's sleek body show.

Like a colour-print of calm Hiroshige
The scene's profound tranquillity,
Foiled dog, blossom, the cat in the tree.
JOSEPH BRADDOCK (b. 1902)

HIGH ON A RIDGE OF TILES

HIGH on a ridge of tiles
A cat, erect and lean,
Looks down and slyly smiles;
The pointed ears are keen,
Listening for a sound
To rise from the backyard.
He casts upon the ground
A moment's cold regard.

Whatever has occurred
Is on so small a scale
That we can but infer
From the trembling of the tail
And the look of blank surprise
That glares out of the eyes
That underneath black fur
His face is deathly pale.
MAURICE JAMES CRAIG (b. 1919)

THREE CAT POEMS

I

ADDRESS OF WELCOME

Like cattle-raiding heroes in the Tain
I've made a kitten-raid across the Boyne;
And you, who lately to your mother clung,
Have travelled far indeed for one so young.

II

OCCASION OF SIN

There's retribution in the Judgment Day
For all who've led an innocent astray.
Each time I leave the room I think of that,
And lock the butter out of reach of cat.

III

THE BOOK OF LIFE

Restored to favour, he's allowed to look
Over my shoulder while I read a book;
Some day, no doubt, I'll be no more than such
And lucky if I understand as much.

MAURICE JAMES CRAIG

THE SHRINE

My silver cat with burning eyes
thinks the wall a paradise
for angling human kind.
She knows the world belongs to her

for her to rend or kill or bless;
the very wind that stirs her fur
she tolerates as a caress
ruffling a can-can glimpse of white
beneath pale argent loveliness.
Intent she concentrates upon
the pilgrim passers-by,
for careless they might miss the sign
of granite sparkling in the sun
that lights her wayside shrine.
The Sphinx-like brindled paws uncurled,
silica-bright her agate unsheathed claws,
hoisted the feather tail unfurled,
exquisite stretch and studied pink-tongued yawn;
thus the arch priestess greets her conquered world.
Worshippers pause in praise and prayer
into that subtle dove-grey fur.
Each thinks he is the only one
soothed and solaced by a purr.
But what is this? Some infidel has brought
a filthy dog into this hallowed street.
Fury stiffens every hair
and fans it like a peacock's tail.
Panache becomes a twitching flail,
and murder broods upon the air.
The stupid dog has scampered by
beneath that lambent amber eye,
ignorant and unaware of it.
His master should have had the wit
to know that even the big green bus
has made this shrine a terminus.

                ETHNA MACCARTHY (*contemporary*)

Nursery Rhymes

PUSSY-CAT MEW

Pussy-cat Mew jumped over a coal,
And in her best petticoat burnt a great hole.
Pussy-cat Mew shall have no more milk
Till she has mended her gown of silk.

KITTY: HOW TO TREAT HER

I like little Pussy, her coat is so warm,
And if I don't hurt her she'll do me no harm;
So I'll not pull her tail, nor drive her away,
But Pussy and I very gently will play.

PUSSY-CAT PUSSY-CAT, WHERE HAVE YOU BEEN?

Pussy-cat, Pussy-cat, where have you been?
—" I've been up to London to look at the Queen."
Pussy-cat, Pussy-cat, what did you there?
—" I frightened a little mouse under her chair."

DING-DONG-BELL

Ding-dong-bell!
Pussy's in the well!
Who put her in?
Little Johnny Thin.
Who pulled her out?
Little Tommy Stout.
What a naughty boy was that
So to drown poor pussy-cat.

PUSSY-CAT, PUSSY-CAT, WHERE ARE YOU GOING?

Pussy-cat, Pussy-cat, where are you going?
"Into the meadow to see the men mowing."
If you go there you are sure to be shot,
Put in a pudding, and boiled in a pot.

TEN LITTLE MICE

Ten little mice sat down to spin;
Pussy passed by, and just looked in,
" What are you doing, my jolly ten? "
" We're making coats for gentlemen."
" Shall I come in and cut your threads?"
" No! No! Mistress Pussy—you'd bite off our heads."

BREAKFAST AND PUSS

Here's my baby's bread and milk,
For her lips as soft as silk;
Here's the basin clean and neat,
Here's the spoon of silver sweet,
Here's the stool, and here's the chair,
For my little lady fair.

No, you must not spill it out,
And drop the bread and milk about;
But let it stand before you flat,
And pray remember pussy-cat:
Poor old pussy-cat that purrs
All so patiently for hers.

True, she runs about the house,
Catching now and then a mouse;
But, though she thinks it very nice,
That only makes a tiny slice:
So don't forget that you should stop
And leave poor puss a little drop.

From " *Rhymes for the Nursery* " (*new edition*, 1839)

THE CRUEL BOY AND THE KITTENS

WHAT! go to see the kittens drowned,
On purpose, in the yard!
I did not think there could be found
A little heart so hard.

Poor kittens! no more pretty play
With pussy's wagging tail:
Oh! I'd go far enough away
Before I'd see the pail.

Poor things! the little child that can
Be pleased to go and see,
Most likely when he grows a man,
A cruel man will be.

And many a wicked thing he'll do,
Because his heart is hard;
A great deal worse than killing you,
Poor kittens, in the yard.

From " Rhymes for the Nursery" (new edition, 1839)

BALLAD OF THE CATS OF BYGONE TIME

Where is the Cat with the Fiddle gone?
The Cats of Kilkenny? The Cheshire? Ah!
Where is the Cat of Dick Whittington?
And Puss-in-Boots, Marquis of Carabas?
In Paradise, or in Nirvana?
Louis Wain's Cats in their ties and spats?
In Lost Atlantis? In Valhalla?
Tell me where is the King of the Cats?

Black, white, yellow, grey, striped, or brown:
Felix the Cat of the Cinema,
The Cat that went up to London Town,
The Cats of Baudelaire (Oh! la! la!),
Fanchette (also from Lutetia),
Where are they hunting for shining rats?
Through what wild nights of Arabia?
Tell me where is the King of the Cats?

Moon-bright Minnaloushe, Pangur Bán,
Tobermory who talked (Aha!),
Tiger-lily, Topaz (my own),
The Cat Hodge (felis Johnsonia):
Crunch they what fishy ambrosia?
Lap they what nectar from creaming vats?
In Tir-n'an-Og? In Arcadia?
Tell me where is the King of the Cats?

Siamese King and Persian Shah!
Cry from your Courts (or your service flats)
Où (dites-moi)—sont tous ces chats?
Tell me where is the King of the Cats?

Michael Scot